The **Essential** Buyer's Guide

JAGUAR

Mark 1 & 2

All models including Daimler 2.5-litre V8 1955 to 1969

Your marque expert:
Nigel Thorley

VELOCE PUBLISHING

THE PUBLISHER OF FINE AUTOMOTIVE BOOKS

Also from Veloce –

Veloce's Essential Buyer's Guide Series
Alfa GT (Booker)
Alfa Romeo Spider Giulia (Booker & Talbott)
Austin Seven (Barker)
BMW GS (Henshaw)
BSA Bantam (Henshaw)
BSA 500 & 650 Twins (Henshaw)
Citroën 2CV (Paxton)
Citroën ID & DS (Heilig)
Corvette C2 1963-1967 (Falconer)
Fiat 500 & 600 (Bobbitt)
Ford Capri (Paxton)
Harley-Davidson Big Twins (Henshaw)
Hinckley Triumph triples & fours 750, 900, 955, 1000, 1050,
   1200 – 1991-2009 (Henshaw)
Honda CBR600 (Henshaw)
Honda FireBlade (Henshaw)
Honda SOHC fours 1969-1984 (Henshaw)
Jaguar E-type 3.8 & 4.2-litre (Crespin)
Jaguar E-type V12 5.3-litre (Crespin)
Jaguar XJ 1995-2003 (Crespin)
Jaguar XK8 (1996-2005) (Thorley)
Jaguar/Daimler XJ6, XJ12 & Sovereign (Crespin)
Jaguar/Daimler XJ40 (Crespin)
Jaguar Mark 2 (1955 to 1969) (Thorley)
Jaguar XJ-S (Crespin)
Land Rover Series I, II & IIA (Thurman)
MGB & MGB GT (Williams)
Mercedes-Benz 280SL-560DSL Roadsters (Bass)
Mercedes-Benz 'Pagoda' 230SL, 250SL & 280SL Roadsters
   & Coupés (Bass)
MG Midget & A-H Sprite (Horler)
MG TD, TF & TF1500 (Jones)
Mini (Paxton)
Morris Minor & 1000 (Newell)
Norton Commando (Henshaw)
Peugeot 205 GTi (Blackburn)
Porsche 911 (964) (Streather)
Porsche 911 (993) (Streather)
Porsche 911 (996) (Streather)
Porsche 911SC (Streather)
Porsche 928 (Hemmings)
Rolls-Royce Silver Shadow & Bentley T-Series (Bobbitt)
Subaru Impreza (Hobbs)
Triumph Bonneville (Henshaw)
Triumph Spitfire & GT6 (Baugues)
Triumph Stag (Mort & Fox)

Triumph TR6 (Williams)
Triumph TR7 & TR8 (Williams)
Vespa Scooters – Classic two-stroke models 1960-2008
   (Paxton)
VW Beetle (Cservenka & Copping)
VW Bus (Cservenka & Copping)
VW Golf GTI (Cservenka & Copping)

From Veloce Publishing's new imprints:

BATTLE CRY!

Soviet General and field rank officer uniforms: 1955 to
   1991 (Streather)
Soviet military and paramilitary services: female
   uniforms 1941-1991 (Streather)

Hubble Hattie

Animal Grief – How animals mourn for each other (Alderton)
Clever Dog! (O'Meara)
Complete Dog Massage Manual, The – Gentle Dog Care
   (Robertson)
Dinner with Rover (Paton-Ayre)
Dog Cookies (Schops)
Dog Games – Stimulating play to entertain your dog and you
   (Blenski)
Dogs on wheels (Mort)
Dog Relax – Relaxed dogs, relaxed owners (Pilguj)
Exercising your puppy: a gentle & natural approach – Gentle
   Dog Care (Robertson)
Fun and games for cats (Seidl)
Know Your Dog – The guide to a beautiful relationship
   (Birmelin)
Living with an Older Dog – Gentle Dog Care (Alderton & Hall)
My dog has cruciate ligament injury – but lives life to the full!
   (Häusler)
My dog has hip dysplasia – but lives life to the full! (Häusler)
My dog is blind – but lives life to the full! (Horsky)
My dog is deaf – but lives life to the full! (Willms)
Smellorama – nose games for dogs (Theby)
Swim to Recovery: Canine hydrotherapy healing (Wong
Waggy Tails & Wheelchairs (Epp)
Walking the dog – motorway walks for drivers and dogs
   (Rees)
Winston ... the dog who changed my life (Klute)
You and Your Border Terrier – The Essential Guide (Alderton)
You and Your Cockapoo – The Essential Guide (Alderton)

www.veloce.co.uk

First published in August 2011 by Veloce Publishing Limited, Veloce House, Parkway Farm Business Park, Middle
Farm Way, Poundbury, Dorchester, Dorset, DT1 3AR, England. Fax 01305 250479/
e-mail info@veloce.co.uk/web www.veloce.co.uk or www.velocebooks.com.

ISBN: 978-1-845843-60-1 UPC: 6-36847-04360-5

© Nigel Thorley and Veloce Publishing 2011. All rights reserved. With the exception of quoting brief passages for the
purpose of review, no part of this publication may be recorded, reproduced or transmitted by any means, including
photocopying, without the written permission of Veloce Publishing Ltd. Throughout this book logos, model names
and designations, etc, have been used for the purposes of identification, illustration and decoration. Such names are
the property of the trademark holder as this is not an official publication. Readers with ideas for automotive books, or
books on other transport or related hobby subjects, are invited to write to the editorial director of Veloce Publishing
at the above address.

British Library Cataloguing in Publication Data – A catalogue record for this book is available from the British Library.
Typesetting, design and page make-up all by Veloce Publishing Ltd on Apple Mac.
Printed in India by Imprint Digital.

Introduction
– the purpose of this book

The announcement of the 2.4-litre saloon at the British Motor show in 1955, gave Jaguar the opportunity to cultivate a new market for its cars. Postwar models like the flagship Mark VII saloon satisfied the needs of those wanting a large, prestigious car, while the XK sports cars provided the panache of the high-performance, two-seater market sector. The 2.4 offered superb engineering, styling and comfort in a small, economical saloon package.

The first production monocoque (chassisless) body, a new 2483cc configuration of the twin-cam XK power unit, and a price of just £1263 made the 2.4 an attractive alternative to the contemporary Daimler Conquest, Humber Super Snipe, or Armstrong Siddeley 234, and an ideal choice for those wishing to trade up from the likes of the Ford Zodiac or Vauxhall Cresta.

In 1957, the 2.4 was joined by a larger, 3.4-litre engined version, and disc brakes became available, making this model an ideal high-performance saloon for club racing and rallies.

In 1959, the Mark 2 replaced the 2.4 and 3.4, a revised version of the earlier models, with improved external and internal styling plus a wider rear track to improve handling. The addition of a third engine variant – 3.8-litre – made this model the fastest production saloon car in the world at the time.

With the purchase of the Daimler company in 1960, Jaguar needed to introduce a new Daimler model to return the business to profitability. At the time, Daimler produced a refined 2.5-litre V8 engine fitted to its limited production SP250 sports car; this engine, tested in a Jaguar 2.4-litre saloon, proved so good that Jaguar decided, for 1962, to launch a new compact Daimler saloon. Named the 2.5-litre V8, using the Daimler engine within the Jaguar Mark 2 bodyshell, and with subtle styling and trim changes, this car offered an interesting alternative to the equivalent Jaguar models. Offering smooth refinement and a different character to the Jaguar Mark 2, the car catered for a more traditional, 'professional' market.

In 1963, the Mark 2s were joined by the S-types. Utilising the same floorpan, similar dimensions, and some of the Mark 2's trim, the slightly more up-market model S-types were available with either the 3.4- or 3.8-litre engine, and also benefitted from independent rear suspension and a larger boot area.

1966 saw the Mark 2 and the S-type (and the Daimler V8) joined by yet another compact saloon, the Jaguar 420, with a more contemporary four-headlamp frontal treatment and revised trim, and fitted with a 4.2-litre version of the twin-cam engine. This was the first Jaguar to be badge engineered into a Daimler model; the Sovereign.

By 1967, the saloon range was being rationalized; the 3.8 Mark 2 and S-types were being discontinued, and economy trim changes were made to the smaller engined Mark 2 – then badged 240 (discontinued in 1969), and 340 (discontinued in 1968). The Daimler was also rebadged as the V8-250, with fewer trim changes. The 420 and Sovereign soldiered on until 1969, by which time Jaguar had adopted a one-saloon-model policy with the new XJ6.

Thanks
My personal thanks to all those who've contributed to this publication, in particular David Marks and Ken Jenkins for their technical expertise.

Contents

Essential Buyer's Guide™ currency
At the time of publication a BG unit of currency "●" equals approximately £1.00/
US$1.61/Euro 1.15. Please adjust to suit current exchange rates.

1 Is it the right car for you?
– marriage guidance

Tall and short drivers
As the car was designed in the 1950s, and despite its relatively small external dimensions, drivers of all sizes shouldn't experience any issues over legroom or headroom.

Weight of controls
Many of these models will not be equipped with power-assisted steering, so this can be heavy, particularly at slow speeds, but the large steering wheel helps manoeuvrability. Power-assisted brakes were fitted to all models and are responsive. The handbrake isn't the most effective, and isn't ideally situated; it can be knocked off by the driver's leg when entering and exiting the car.

Sporty in nature, but with plenty of driver room. This is a Daimler 2.5-litre V8 with split-bench seats and no centre console area ...

Will it fit in the garage?
2.4/3.4, Mark 2, 240, 340 and Daimler V8
Length: 180.75in 4591mm
Width: 66.75in 1695mm
Height: 57.75in 1467mm

S-type
Length: 187in   4769mm
Width: 66.25in 1683mm
Height: 55.75in 1416mm

420/Sovereign
Length: 187.5in 4762mm
Width: 67in   1702mm
Height: 56.25in 1429mm

Interior space
These cars can only be classed as four-seaters.

... but, like the Mark 2, it is not ideal for a big family or long-legged passengers.

 Seat width is good, as is headroom, although rear seat passengers may notice a lack of legroom, particularly if the front seats are adjusted well back.

Luggage capacity
Boot space is adequate, but hampered by the slope of the boot lid on most models. S-types and 420s benefit from a larger, more usable boot. All models feature door pockets, under-dashboard shelf, and lockable glovebox, the 2.4 and 3.4 also having

5

an open cubby box on the driver's side of the dashboard.

Running costs
These are classic cars and are unlikely to cover a high mileage these days, so normal servicing costs will be relatively low. Servicing every 3000 miles or annually; oil consumption will be dependent on use and condition of the engine, but should certainly be between 300 and 800 miles per pint. Expect to achieve between 19 and 23mpg.

The Mark 2's boot space is acceptable, but the S-type and 420 provide better.

Usability
All are very practical in today's driving conditions, although heating and ventilation aren't the cars' strongest points.

Parts availability
Because of the popularity of the Jaguar marque, and the interchangeability of components between these and other models, there's a plentiful supply of new or reproduction parts for all models. Be wary of some reproduction items; they may not be up to the standard of the original Jaguar versions.

Parts cost
The biggest costs come with bodywork repairs, most of which are down to the labour involved. Jaguar parts are not the cheapest around, and remember that most of these cars had leather upholstery and wood veneer which aren't cheap to replace. These cars are still relatively economical to maintain compared to many other 'exotic' brands.

Insurance
There are a significant number of specialist classic and 'cherished vehicle' policies available, offering very attractive insurance rates for these cars.

Investment potential
Due to a major hyke in all classic car prices in the early 1990s, the Mark 2 models, in particular, reached very high figures, but suffered harshly with the 'crash' that followed. Prices haven't recovered significantly, but properly restored or original examples can certainly fetch good prices, albeit still not equivalent to the actual cost of restoring an example today.

Alternatives
The range of sporting equivalents to these cars is quite limited, but one might consider the Rover P6, Triumph 2000/2.5, Ford Lotus-Cortina, or Vauxhall Ventora. European models include the Mercedes 250SE, Volvo 164, Citroën DS21, Alfa Romeo 2600, BMW 1800Ti, or Lancia Flaminia 2600. Other, more mundane or traditional alternatives are the Rover 3-litre, Ford Zodiac, Vauxhall Cresta, Wolseley 6/110, Vanden Plas Princess, or Humber Super Snipe.

2 Cost considerations
– affordable, or a money pit?

A reasonable Mark 2, with the smaller 2.4-litre engine and disc wheels. Unmodified it can make an ideal economical purchase.

Don't consider a basket case unless you've the time, patience, and money to survive it!

Purchase price
As with any classic car, buying the best car you can afford is certainly true with these cars. Consider the amount of time and money that needs to be put into a car, compared to buying one properly restored or still essentially original.

Expect to spend over ●20,000 for an excellent example that you can use and show straight away, but, even then, expect to have some work to do. If you want the very best, expect to pay a lot more. Alternatively, buying a much cheaper example will leave you with cash to do the work in stages, if you've sufficient funds to see the project through. Remember: in most cases, your budget for a refurbishment/restoration is likely to be exceeded. Nearly everything mechanical can be addressed quite easily, but bodywork is the most expensive and time-consuming aspect of any work.

These cars are still very prone to corrosion.

Servicing
Typical intervals are: basic oil change; 3000 miles or annually if lesser mileage. Full service; 6000 miles or annually if lesser mileage. Major service; 12,000 to 18,000 miles dependent on usage. Brake fluid change; two years.

Parts price (approximate)
Brake pads ●x20 per axle set
Brake discs ●x25 each
Brake master cylinder ●x100
Brake servo ●x250 exchange
Head gasket set ●x63
Gearbox rebuild ●x1000
Fuel pump ●x70
Exhaust System (stainless) ●x400
Radiator ●x225
Clutch kit set ●x175
Dynamo ●x70 exchange
Water pump ●x80
Shock absorbers ●x100 per set of 4

Carburettor repair kit ●x50
Starter motor ●x80 exchange
Front crossmember ●x65
Crows foot ●x25
Front wing section repair ●x280
Sill panel ●x115
Door skin (front) ●x65
Door skin (rear) ●x80
Complete interior wood veneer refurbishment ●x1150
Headlining trim kit ●x165
Complete carpet set ●x400
Complete leather trim set ●x2000

Used parts
Available particularly through specialist dismantlers and at autojumbles, or through the Jaguar club magazines.

3 Living with a Jaguar Mark 1 or 2
– will you get along together?

Living with one of these cars can be a real joy. This is a 1958 3.4 Mark 1.

Good points
Good looks
Classic status
Instantly recognisable
Performance and economy (for the period)
Luxury and prestige
Reasonable accommodation
Good parts and support back-up
Easy maintenance
Lots of modern updates available

Bad points
Corrosion
Cost of restoration
Poor heating and ventilation
Rear legroom
Some component costs

Summary
Beautiful, curvaceous styling that everyone appreciates. Excellent performance, good long-legged cruiser – particularly with overdrive – and a car to really enjoy driving on the road or track.

4 Relative values
– which model for you?

Models

There's a strong differential in price for these cars, dependent on condition and the desirability of a particular model.

The list below provides approximate values between the various models based on 100% being the most desirable model, with the others shown as a percentage of that value. These percentages don't, however, take into account particularly rare (original, ultra-low mileage) examples, those with important provenance, or cars in award-winning concours condition. These will command even higher prices.

What, for many, is the ultimate model – the 3.8-litre Mark 2, in Carmen Red and with chrome wire wheels.

The early 2.4- and 3.4-litre models (now known as Mark 1s) are something of an acquired taste, and

have a traditional look and 1950s feel that makes them unusual and appealing, as well as being the rarest of the breed. Their biggest downsides are the narrow rear track, which can make for spirited handling, and the somewhat claustrophobic look, with a smaller glass area.

The Mark 2 is, stylistically, the most appealing and instantly recognisable. The 3.8-litre engined car is the top performer and the most sought after model. Saving money, a 3.4-litre version still offers excellent performance, while the 2.4-litre provides the looks and feel without the speed or acceleration.

At the lower end of the price scale, but nevertheless a real classic Jaguar, the 240 has the benefit of a straight port cylinder head.

240 and 340 models are the least desirable, because most don't have leather upholstery. Some of the trim was downgraded to keep the price

For a better ride and more boot space, there's the S-type on the left, or with the bigger 4.2-litre engine, the 420 on the right.

competitive, in the final years of production, so these cars can represent excellent value for money and could be upgraded with better trim.

The Daimler V8s have a charm and character all their own. Not known for outright performance, they're very refined, and a rare manual transmission version is a treat to drive.

S-types and 420s are a compromise in styling, yet offer better handling and ride, with independent rear suspension and a bigger boot. The 420 also offers the larger 4235cc version of the XK engine, with better torque.

Values

3.8-litre Mark 2	**100%**
3.4-litre Mark 2	**85%**
3.8-litre S-type	**65%**
3.4-litre (Mark 1)	**62%**
340	**60%**
3.4-litre S-type	**55%**
2.4-litre Mark 2	**50%**
420	**48%**
Daimler 2.5-litre V8	**48%**
Daimler V8-250	**46%**
Daimler 420 Sovereign	**45%**
2.4-litre (Mark 1)	**45%**
240	**42%**

All the above prices are based on manual/overdrive models (except for the Daimler V8s). Manual transmission

Jaguar Mark 2 looks, but with a silky smooth V8 engine and a cheaper price tag; the Daimlers are worth considering.

Daimler V8s are rare and will command values up to **20%** higher.

Other models with automatic transmission will command prices around **5%** lower.

Often overlooked by buyers, the 2.4-litre (Mark 1) offers period looks and traditional Jaguar values, but at a lower price.

5 Before you view
– be well informed

To avoid a wasted journey, and the disappointment of finding that the car doesn't match your expectations, be very clear about what questions you want to ask before you pick up the telephone. Some of these points might appear basic, but when you're excited about the prospect of buying your dream classic, it's amazing how some of the most obvious things slip the mind. Also, check classic car magazines for the current values of the model you are interested, which give both a price guide and auction results.

Where is the car?
Is it going to be worth travelling to the next county, state, or even another country? A locally advertised car, although it may not sound very interesting, can add to your knowledge for very little effort, so make a visit – it might even be in better condition than expected.

Dealer or private sale?
Establish early on if the car is being sold by its owner or by a trader. A private owner should have all the history, so don't be afraid to ask detailed questions.

A dealer may have more limited knowledge of a car's history, but should have some documentation. A dealer may offer a warranty/guarantee (ask for a printed copy) and finance.

Cost of collection and delivery?
A dealer may well be used to quoting for delivery by car transporter. A private owner may agree to meet you halfway, but only agree to this after you have seen the car at the vendor's address to validate the documents. Conversely, you could meet halfway and agree the sale, but insist on meeting at the vendor's address for the handover.

View – when and where?
It's always preferable to view at the vendors home or business premises. In the case of a private sale, the car's documentation should tally with the vendor's name and address. Arrange to view only in daylight and avoid a wet day: most cars look better in poor light or when wet.

Reason for sale?
Do make this one of the first questions. Why is the car being sold, and how long has it been with the current owner? How many previous owners?

Left-hand drive to right-hand drive
Many of these models will have been re-imported into the UK, or transferred from the UK to overseas countries. If a steering conversion has been carried out, it may reduce the value, and it may well be that other aspects of the car still reflect the specification for a foreign market; this may affect the legality of the car. The chassis number will confirm whether the car was originally rhd or lhd.

Condition (body/chassis/interior/mechanicals)?

Ask for an honest appraisal of the car's condition. Ask specifically about some of the check items described in chapter 7.

All original specification?

An original equipment car is invariably of higher value than a customised version.

Matching data/legal ownership

All these cars carry chassis, body, engine, and gearbox numbers. Do all these numbers and the licence plate match the official registration document? Engine numbers are stamped on the block and (except for the 420) on the cylinder head, so they should match. Chassis numbers are stamped on the body panel ahead of the radiator; is this the same as on the chassis plate and on the log book? If the chassis number ends in the letters 'BW,' this indicates an automatic transmission model, and a 'P' prefix indicates the car was originally fitted with power-assisted steering; in both cases, compare with the actual equipment on the car. Top prices are commanded for cars with all these numbers and equipment

The way the wipers park is a pointer to a lhd to rhd conversion.

Ask about originality. This 2.4-litre Mark 1's gear lever is wrong, as is the gaiter, and the kick board is damaged with the fitting of a modern audio speaker; all affect the car's value.

Does the car have matching numbers corresponding to this data plate?

matching, although with the age of the vehicles it's inevitable that some changes may have occurred.

Is the owner's name and address recorded in the official registration documents?

For those countries that require an annual test of roadworthiness, does the car have a document showing it complies (an MoT certificate in the UK, which can be verified on 0845 600 5977)?

Chassis numbers on most of these cars are stamped on the panel ahead of the radiator, as shown in this 240.

If a smog/emissions certificate is mandatory, does the car have one?

If required, does the car carry a current road fund licence/licence plate tag?

Does the vendor own the car outright? Money might be owed to a finance company or bank: the car could even be stolen. Several organisations will supply the data on ownership, based on the car's licence plate number, for a fee. Such companies can often also tell you whether the car has been 'written-off' by an insurance company. In the UK the following organisations can supply vehicle data:

HPI – 01722 422 422
AA – 0870 600 0836
DVLA – 0870 240 0010
RAC – 0870 533 3660
Other countries will have similar organisations.

Unleaded fuel
If necessary, has the car been modified to run on unleaded fuel?

Insurance?
Check with your existing insurer before setting out; your current policy might not cover you to drive the car if you do purchase it.

How you can pay
A cheque will take several days to clear, and the seller may prefer to sell to a cash buyer. However, a banker's draft (a cheque issued by a bank) is as good as cash, but safer, so contact your own bank and become familiar with the formalities that are necessary to obtain one.

Buying at auction?
If the intention is to buy at auction see chapter 10 for further advice.

Professional vehicle check (mechanical examination)?
There are marque/model specialists who will undertake a professional examination of a vehicle on your behalf. Owners' clubs will be able to put you in touch with such specialists.

Other organisations that will carry out a general professional check in the UK are:
AA – 0800 085 3007
ABS – 0800 358 5855
RAC – 0870 533 3660
Again, other countries will have organisations offering similar services.

6 Inspection equipment
– these items will really help

Before you rush out of the door, gather together a few items that will help as you work your way around the car.

There's no substitute for taking someone along with you who knows these cars well.

This book
This book is designed to be your guide at every step, so take it along and use the check boxes to help you assess each area of the car you're interested in. Don't be afraid to let the seller see you using it.

Reading glasses (if you need them for close work)
Take your reading glasses if you need them to read documents and make close up inspections.

Magnet (not powerful, a fridge magnet is ideal)

A magnet will help you check if the car is full of filler from previous, cheap repairs. Use the magnet to sample bodywork areas all around the car, but be careful not to damage the paintwork. Expect to find a little filler here and there, but not whole panels.

Torch

A torch with fresh batteries will be useful for peering into the wheelarches and under the car.

Probe (a small screwdriver works very well)

A small screwdriver can be used – with care – as a probe, particularly on the underside. With this you should be able to check any areas of severe corrosion, but be careful – if it's really bad the screwdriver might go right through the metal!

Overalls

Be prepared to get dirty. Take along a pair of overalls, if you have them.

Mirror on a stick

Fixing a mirror at an angle on the end of a stick may seem odd, but you'll probably need it to check the condition of the underside of the car. It will also help you to peer into some of the important crevices. You can also use it, together with the torch, along the underside of the sills and on the floor. You're looking for accident damage, as well as corrosion.

Digital camera

If you have the use of a digital camera, take it along so that later you can study some areas of the car more closely. Take a picture of any part of the car that causes you concern, and seek a friend's opinion.

A friend, preferably a knowledgeable enthusiast

Ideally, have a friend or knowledgeable enthusiast accompany you: a second opinion is always valuable.

7 Fifteen minute evaluation
– walk away or stay?

These particular models are well balanced, curvaceous, and dripping in chrome, so it's very easy to be taken aback by the looks, a shiny paint finish, and a nice exhaust note!

Buying any classic car is partly down to emotion, as well as price. However, buying one of these cars 'right' is crucial to your wallet and well-being, so this book will help you through the whole process. However, there's no substitute for more knowledge, so if you can enlist the help of an expert who knows these models well, it may well prevent you from making the wrong decision; costing you much heartache and money.

Your initial check should cover the basics, such as paperwork and provenance, the rest is down to the type of car you're looking for.

Concours contender

If your choice and pocket is for a concours or near concours car, one would think you could take many aspects for granted, but that's not the case. Just as beauty is in the eye of the beholder, so the word 'concours' means different things to different people, and all owners tend to look at their cars through rose tinted spectacles.

If the car you're looking at is truly concours, it will have supporting documentation (paperwork, certificates, pictures, prizes, etc), and that doesn't mean a simple plastic trophy for a 'peoples choice' in a local car show. To be absolutely sure of how good such a car really is, you need the support of an experienced concours judge, and the

A true concours car will have lots of proof that it has competed and achieved success.

criteria for such a model. The devil is in the detail, and it isn't just a matter of how clean the components are, but also if they're correct for that model and year of manufacture: being able to identify what's right and wrong with a 'concours' example is beyond the scope of this book.

One of the most problematic issues relates to originality, as so many people over the years have modified their cars, either because they didn't know better, couldn't find the right parts, wanted to save money, or to suit individual needs. Even such items as changing the steering wheel, or the fitting of different wheels, will mean extra costs over the top-end price such cars can command (if you want to put such matters right). To be a true concours contender, such

What a concours engine bay should look like, in this case a 240 model.

cars need to have ALL their original equipment, like, for example, the comprehensive tool kit (now a very expensive item to source and buy).

Then there are the issues relating to restoration. Are the panel gaps good and consistent? Are there any (even minor) signs of poor paintwork, corrosion coming through, or pitted chrome? Does the engine sound as good as it looks, and does the car actually drive well, another common problem even with concours cars?

A genuine, nice classic

A more moderately priced car still requires a great deal of attention, particularly in the fifteen minute evaluation. This will determine if the car is genuine or if the degree of remedial work puts it into the next categories (daily driver, or complete but needing work).

Such cars should be well prepared, have good body and paintwork, a nice interior, and be mechanically excellent. Don't expect a faultless body; stone chips, some remedial paintwork, etc, are acceptable. In this category you're looking for a really good car that does everything it's supposed to do, but may not be 'mint.'

A perfectly acceptable genuine engine bay, in this case a 2.4-litre Mark 1, with Solex carburettors. Inner wings are the wrong colour; has the exterior been repainted?

A daily driver

With such moderately priced cars, don't expect the best, but you can still check fundamental items like matching numbers: although not that important for a daily driver, if the car has a different engine or transmission, this can help with price negotiations.

The fundamental issues are that such cars are mechanically and bodily sound, have a long MoT, and are presentable, so making for a reliable classic. Even better, get the seller to agree to you acquiring a new MoT at a garage of your choice.

Complete but needing work

The biggest issue here is ensuring good bodywork initially. This is the most important part of the car, as these monocoque construction vehicles are

This 420 was a daily driver, but it looks as if it has been standing for some time and been messed around with.

highly prone to corrosion and, at their worst, can be terminal. The other matter is the word 'complete'; if anything is off the car in boxes, is it all there?

Ensure you have adequate insurance before taking the car for a test drive.

The road test

Ensuring you've adequate insurance cover, it's vital you road test any car you're considering purchasing. This should be agreed with the owner prior to viewing, asking him, if practical, not to warm the engine, allowing you to start it from cold.

In the driver's seat, ensure all the usual controls that you'll need work correctly, including steering wheel and mirror adjustment. Except for modified examples, the 2.4-litre and V8 models, all these cars had an automatic choke. Turn on the ignition, push the starter button, and lower the driver's window so you can listen to the engine as it ticks over. If you're not accustomed to these engines, a loud 'hissing' indicates that the automatic choke is working. Listen for any rattles or other noises from the engine area, or blowing from the exhaust system. Engine rattles on start-up could be attributable to timing chain issues, piston slap, or worse. If the engine sounds 'flat' when starting, this could just be down to poor battery condition.

A quick glance through the rear view mirror should determine whether haze or blue smoke is coming from the exhaust, indicating engine problems. Check the instrument warning lights for any sign of trouble, and the instruments for oil pressure (a minimum 60psi on tickover with a cold engine), and battery condition/charge, etc.

The engine should be ticking over smoothly and quietly, and as the temperature rises, the automatic choke should cut off, allowing the engine to tick over at an indicated 800rpm on the rev counter. At this point, press the brake pedal to get a feel for the servo-assisted brakes, to ensure pedal pressure isn't too hard or pedal travel too long.

Try some of the important controls like lighting, wipers, indicators, and horn to ensure they all work correctly. Also try the window winders and seat adjustment.

The oil pressure gauge on the Mark 1 is very accurate. This is a good reading on tickover, with 'normal' water temperature as shown.

If an automatic transmission model, depress the brake pedal and engage 'drive,' noting any harshness or excessive noise that may indicate incorrect adjustment (or worse with the transmission). If a manual transmission, depress the clutch and engage first gear. The earlier cars were equipped with a gearbox with a non-synchromesh long-throw first gear, later cars having an all-synchromesh unit. Both these gearboxes are very strong, but gear selection can be a little 'stodgy,' which is normal.

Moving off on the road test, there should be no clutch judder and gear changes should be smooth, if a little slow. If equipped with overdrive, this only operates in top gear so, when above a speed of around 35mph, ensure it engages and disengages smoothly. With the three-speed automatic transmission, (although quite 'ancient' by modern standards), changes up and down should be smooth, and it's worth trying the 'kickdown' (either from a standstill or at very slow speeds) by flooring the accelerator. This should allow the transmission to drop a gear and as you continue to accelerate hard – road conditions permitting – gear changes will occur later and relatively smoothly.

The ride shouldn't be harsh or sloppy. Try to drive the car on varying road surfaces and at differing speeds to test for wheel balance and overall smoothness. These cars can be prone to a fair degree of wind noise, which isn't indicative of a problem. Ideally, a 20 mile round trip is the best option to get a true feel for the car. Excessive sloppiness in the steering, suspension knocks, groans, or scraping of the wheels within the wheelarches all indicate problems to be investigated. Also, listen for rattling exhaust systems.

As the engine warms up, check the water temperature gauge, which should read no more than mid-point, and also re-check oil pressure. Ideally, an engine should run at an absolute minimum of 40psi at between 2500 and 3000rpm, and certainly at no less than 25-30psi on tickover.

The brakes should be progressive and operate evenly and, despite the weight of these cars, as they are discs all round (except for a few 2.4s and 3.4s), they should be perfectly capable of stopping the car quickly in today's traffic conditions. The handbrake was never that efficient, but should hold the car on a reasonable slope; problems are usually down to incorrect adjustment or their general inefficiency.

It's also worth stopping on occasion, switching off the engine, and re-starting, looking for blue smoke from behind, rattles, or any hesitancy in starting.

Checks back at base

Once you've established from the road test that you want to investigate further, the next stage is to return to base and check other areas.

Engine bay

If an automatic, with the engine still running, the handbrake on, and the footbrake applied, cycle through the D and L positions. With the engine idling, check the automatic transmission oil level via the dipstick in the engine bay. From this you can not only check the level, but also the condition of the oil. If the oil is brown instead of red, or has an intense burnt smell, this is an indication of poor maintenance and, possibly, problems to come.

With the engine still running and now fully warmed, listen for top-end timing chain rattle from the front of the engine. These XK power units are relatively quiet but should emit a small amount of

Don't worry about the dirt; it will show up any fluid leaks. Here, one hose is imploding, the other is split.

tappet noise, although nothing excessive. Check around the engine bay for obvious fluid leaks, check the condition of the radiator, battery, and other ancillaries, but don't concern yourself if it's not absolutely clean and spotless (unless you're looking at a concours example). Look and listen for leaks from the exhaust manifold, check for any petrol fumes from the carburetors or fuel pipes, and look for any signs of corrosion on the inner wings or bulkhead (particularly behind the battery).

A quick check of the visible parts of the main wiring loom is worthwhile, as removal and replacement with a new one is an expensive process.

Bodywork and interior

Is the body panel fit good and consistent? A cursory look along the flanks of the body will indicate undulations and poor shaping from repairs. The door rubbers are visible from the outside; are they covered in paint from resprays?

The sill of this Mark 2 is 'flat' with filler where it meets the bottom of the front wing, and the door skin doesn't fit flush.

Side light pods are lead loaded. The bottom right is just starting to 'lift.' Note the discolouration of the lens.

Removing the rear seat reveals the floorpan. This one is quite good, apart from the splitting near the transmission tunnel.

Are there any significant rust bubbles appearing, or movement of the lead loading from around the side light pods on the Mark 2 wings? Are the jacking points intact? A cursory look underneath the car, and under the carpets inside the car, should reveal any corrosion issues. Finally, lift out the back seat squab to check the condition of the rear floopan area – a common, and sometimes terminal, area of corrosion.

A severe case of badly fitted door rubbers. The front one is difficult to replace without removing the door from the car, so this one was painted over.

With the interior, check the general condition of the trim; have any later mods been added, like modern audio equipment, extra speakers, and other non-original items, that will have damaged the trim. Are under-dash panels intact, are the door trim panels damaged from ingress of water, and are the carpets in reasonable condition?

In the boot, unclip and remove the Hardura matting, and remove the spare wheel cover and wheel to view the inside of the spare wheel well. This will give a good indication of corrosion and previous repairs.

Even without removing the spare wheel, the underfloor area of this S-type looks excellent and original.

8 Key points
– where to look for problems

There are two key issues probably more important than any others when considering the purchase of one of these models, for the obvious reason of cost.

The single biggest issue relates to the body, which is quite complex. When it was conceived in the 1950s, little thought was given to protection and longevity, compared with today's cars. With no chassis, the whole body forms the structure of the vehicle, so it's vital it's in good condition. Don't be fooled by a nice paint job and no obvious signs of corrosion. Even a restored car may harbour signs of a poor repair or 'cover up.'

I'm not suggesting you go to this extreme; simply pulling back carpets can reveal the condition of the floorpan.

Here, from the underside, the extent of floorpan corrosion can easily be seen.

Showing just how vulnerable these cars are to corrosion: you can't see these areas until a body is dismantled!

All the bodies, regardless of model, are based on the same principle floopan with complex strengthening members. This floorpan is the first area to check, particularly around the extreme edges where it meets the inner sills, at the rear, under the rear seat pan, and on the Mark 1s, Mark 2s, 240/340s, and V8s, underneath, where the channel is formed to take the Panhard rod connection to the rear axle. Similarly, the radius arm mountings (one per side), that attach the independent rear suspension to the floorpan on the S-types and 420s. Other areas of corrosion

The Panhard rod mounting is particularly vulnerable, affecting Mark 1, Mark 2, 240/340, and Daimler V8s.

Body filler can hide a multitude of sins, like this oil can repair!

and repair (which will be mentioned later), although time-consuming and possibly expensive to repair, aren't insurmountable. Indeed, new complete or repaired panels are easily available for the Mark 2 variants. However, some panels, like front wings and complete rear wings for the other models aren't.

The other major area of concern is the engine. Whilst, mechanically, nearly everything is available for these cars, a Jaguar XK or Daimler V8 engine rebuild doesn't come cheap. In view of the weight, and the awkward nature of removal and refitting within a confined area, it's not the easiest job to do at home, even given the correct equipment and expertise. A complete engine rebuild will set you back thousands.

9 Serious evaluation

– 30 minutes for years of enjoyment

Score each section according to the values in the boxes: 4 = excellent; 3 = good; 2 = average; 1 = poor. Major items have higher values, shown in the relevant boxes. The totting up procedure is detailed at the end of the chapter. Be realistic in your marking!

You've got this far, so now it's time to go for the step-by-step detailed inspection, before deciding whether to part with your hard earned cash. Read, digest, check against your intended purchase and then tick the appropriate box (excellent, good, average or poor) and total the points. Be vigilant over the key pointers first highlighted in chapter 8.

Overall stance

Start with the obvious: how does the car sit? Sagging at the front? With conventional wheels and tyres, there should be at least 2½in of space between the top of the tyre and the uppermost edge of the wheelarch. Although the rear end can appear deceptive, because of the shape of the rear wings (and spats in the case of some of the models), it shouldn't be so low that the tyres scrape the wheelarches under load. The car should be nearly level or slightly down at the rear.

General stance should be very slightly rear-end down – this S-type obviously has weak front springs.

Paintwork 4 3 2 1

Very few cars still have their original paint finish. The better the paint finish, the better the car will look, and the more professional the work that will have been done. Look, particularly, for overspray on areas like chrome, rubbers, and on the inside of door shut faces. Compare the colour of the car with that of any hidden areas, which will confirm if the car has had a colour change.

Correct ride height gap between the top of the front wheel and the wheelarch.

An ideal check is to fold down the centre instrument panel by undoing the two knurled knobs. Inside you'll see the innermost area of the bulkhead, which won't have been repainted unless a complete restoration has been carried out, with the bodywork stripped.

Although the whole dashboard has been removed here, with all the cars except the Mark 1, the centre dash section can be folded down to reveal the bodywork behind; an excellent place to confirm the original colour of the car.

Easy to tell a good body, with every panel equally gapped and smooth lines throughout.

Check the wheelarch lips for debris and filler.

A door removed from a car for repair. The yellow horizontal line shows where the outer skins are cut to replace the panel. On poorly repaired examples, welded-in areas can be seen through the paint.

Body panels

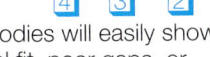

The gentle curvature of these bodies will easily show up any imperfections, bad panel fit, poor gaps, or bulges where repairs have been carried out.

Starting at the front of the car, are the complex wings in good condition, looking particularly at the side light housings in the Mark 2, 240/340 and Daimler V8 models on top of the wings? These are separate items welded and lead loaded in place; usually the first places to show problems with either the lead 'giving,' or corrosion coming through. Feel around the front wheelarch lips. If repairs have been carried out here, are the edges bent over? Otherwise, scraping can be caused by the tyres under harsh braking. Are the wheelarch lips clear of road debris, or shaped with filler? Look across the line of the wings from the front of the car; if repair sections have been worked into the wings, the welding and filling shouldn't be detectable.

Next, open the bonnet and check the condition of the inside edges, an area often missed when wax protecting.

Moving to the side of the car, look at the line of the sills to the bottom edges of the front wings and door bottoms, where the sills mate to the back wings on the S-type/420, and to the spats on the other models. To get the general curvature correct, and to ensure

Underbonnet inspection (in this case an S-type) can reveal a lot, like fluid leaks, rusty components and corroded bonnets.

joins between welded panels were hidden, Jaguar (and good restorers) used lead loading; a time-consuming job, but, if done professionally in the later life of the car, this should ensure a near perfect line, with no marks or undulations anywhere. The shape of these bodies makes it difficult to get all the lines correct, but once they are, this is indicative of either originality or excellent later workmanship that will always pay dividends.

Next, check the bottoms of the doors for repairs or where skins have been replaced. These must be done with the doors off the car, so looking at the forward shut faces of the door frames (where the hinges are) will show any bodged repairs. The bottoms of the doors are prone to rusting out due to build up of water, so this is an ideal place to use your magnet to identify proper steel repairs. Check to see if the metal plates are still intact

With the rear doors open, access is gained to the two 'deutz' fasteners that secure the rear spats in place.

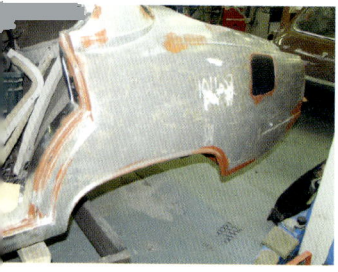

Rear wings for S-types and 420s are very difficult to come by.

underneath the doors; these direct away water that drains from above. Look at the top curved area of the outer door panels, below the chrome trim level. Many repairers fit part-skins here, so any undulations, ripples, or marks might indicate poor welding.

At the rear, the spats are easily removable by undoing two Deutz fasteners, accessible with the rear doors open. It's worthwhile removing these spats to check their condition, and provide better visibility to the rear wheelarch areas. The rear wings are particularly susceptible to corrosion caused by debris thrown up from the wheels. The wheelarch lips on the S-type/420s are particularly vulnerable, as is the lower section of the other models wings. At the rear, the boot lid is vulnerable to corrosion at its base, where the skin is peened over. With the boot open, check the condition of the rear wheelarches. It's an ideal opportunity, particularly with the larger booted S-types and 420s, to unscrew the side panels and remove them to see inside the wings, and more of the wheelarch section. On the S-types and 420s, this is where the twin fuel tanks are housed, so check their condition, too. The wheelarches are more visible on the other models, but the side panels can also be easily removed, providing good visibility to the wing innards.

The rear spats normally fitted to later Mark 1, Mark 2, 240/340, and Daimler V8 models are prone to corrosion. This Mark 1 shows the narrower rear track of that model.

Removing the boot side panels reveals much of the internal bodywork for corrosion inspection. Except for S-types/420s, which have twin fuel tanks, all the cars have their fuel pumps here, on the left.

Chrome and other trim

There's a lot of chrome plating on these models, and refurbishment can be very expensive indeed. Items, such as the door frames (except for the Mark 1s), were chromed on a brass base, as were the radiator grilles, so these will last better. Other areas, like the

Comparison between the Mark 1 (left) and Mark 2 door construction.

Door handles are Mazak, so don't re-chrome well. Window surrounds are also 'delicate.'

Bumpers are expensive to re-chrome; boot plinths and light housings are Mazak.

bumper bars and overriders, will also fare well, but, because of their size, are costly to re-chrome or repair if dented or rusted. Most other bright trim is chromed on Mazak (or monkey metal, as it's commonly known), a cast metal that deteriorates badly, showing signs of pitting. Usually, this cannot be re-chromed effectively, so replacements are required; these include the door handles, leaper mascots, rear light units, and rear number plate plinths.

Check the condition of the front windscreen and rear screen rubbers, and their chrome surrounds. The rubbers are replaceable but, in some cases, like the windscreen of the Mark 1 models, for example, it has to be removed from the inside, and this means dislodging the headlining. The chrome screen surrounds should be in good condition and fit snugly. Not only are they difficult to replace, they're also fragile, and later reproduction replacements aren't that good. With the glass, check for bad scratching, or delaminating in the case of a laminated screen.

An easy method of identifying the age of the car is by the etching on the glass.

All the windows should have etched markings from the manufacturer, with the added benefit of indicating the age of the glass, which should tie in with the age of the car. Most will carry the word 'toughened' on the glass with a very small dot below one of the letters. This indicates the year of manufacture so, for example, a dot below the 'T' (the first letter) means 1961, and one below the 'D' would indicate a zero; a dot below the second 'E' means eight or 1968 . Some cars will have been fitted with a heated rear screen, either operated automatically when the heater fan is switched on, or by a manual dashboard-mounted switch: check that it still works.

Check all of the lights to ensure they are corrosion-free. All have chrome surrounds, so check their condition as it's probably better to buy complete replacement units rather than attempt to re-chrome the plinths. While many of the light units

Check that the heated screens work on cars so equipped.

Light units differ on each model and are special to the car (some are 'handed') so, even if the lenses look common to other vehicles, the plinths are not.

were a contemporary fit to other cars, the side lights for the Mark 1 are totally unique, and the rear light housings may look the same as many others, but the plinths are actually a different shape in order to mate to the curvature of the rear wings.

The door seals are an important area; not only do they prevent wind noise, they also form a seal against the ingress of water and, in the case of these models, have an aesthetic aspect. They're always visible between the panel gaps, so they must be in good condition. Also, the front door seals on the A posts are secured behind a riveted panel that is very difficult to access: the seals are very difficult to fit unless the front doors are removed from the car – another sign of 'proper' work having being done.

There's also a seal on the scuttle ventilator ahead of the windscreen, at the rear of the bonnet area. Check that this is intact, along with the mesh panel that prevents the ingress of foreign bodies.

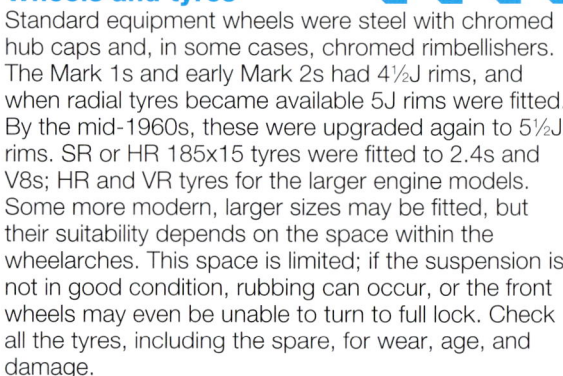

The front doors have to be removed to gain access to fit new door seals correctly.

Wheel sizes varied throughout production, as did hub caps; in this case post-1967 240/340 type with optional rimbellishers.

Wheels and tyres 4 3 2 1

Standard equipment wheels were steel with chromed hub caps and, in some cases, chromed rimbellishers. The Mark 1s and early Mark 2s had 4½J rims, and when radial tyres became available 5J rims were fitted. By the mid-1960s, these were upgraded again to 5½J rims. SR or HR 185x15 tyres were fitted to 2.4s and V8s; HR and VR tyres for the larger engine models. Some more modern, larger sizes may be fitted, but their suitability depends on the space within the wheelarches. This space is limited; if the suspension is not in good condition, rubbing can occur, or the front wheels may even be unable to turn to full lock. Check all the tyres, including the spare, for wear, age, and damage.

Many cars were, or have been later fitted with wire wheels (silver or body colour painted, or chromed) on splined hubs. It's vital to check the condition of these wheels and splines; if they're worn, serious problems

The condition of the hub splines on wire wheeled cars is important. Damage here can clearly be seen.

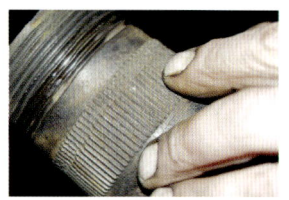

may arise. By tapping each spoke, you can tell if any are loose or damaged; they should produce a metallic 'ring' if they are okay. Look for rim damage from curbing, and, if practical, remove each wheel to check the condition of the splines, both on the wheels themselves and on the hubs. At the very least, rock the car near each wheel, checking for any movement of the wheels on the hubs.

Underside

Given that a cursory check on the most important areas was carried out with your fifteen minute evaluation, the same areas should now be checked in greater detail.

In many cases, the underside will have been treated with underseal or wax protection, so it's important to check all areas carefully, particularly where there appears to be an excess of underseal; it could be hiding a poor repair – or no repair at all. Work your way methodically from front to rear, tapping the bodywork, carefully prodding with a screwdriver, looking for problems.

A crossmember spans the entire width of the car, at the front behind the bumper, and, at each end, a perforated panel (commonly known as crows feet) is attached. Check all these for condition as they are a regular problem area for corrosion (replacement panels are available). Check the chassis legs, and,

Underneath at the front, the crow's feet as they are called (for obvious reasons), and the front crossmember are prone to corrosion.

Checking the floorpan from inside the car, by lifting the carpets and underlay.

while you are there, all the V and sandwich mountings. Check all four jacking points for rust and security. Check the seams of the floorpan where they mate with the inner and outer sills, and re-check the floorpan itself, especially around the rear seating area where it lifts over the back axle. Re-check all the wheelarches for corrosion and repairs. Inspect more carefully the mounting

A typical find in the rear wheelarch, but fortunately, in this case, not serious corrosion.

Jacking points are well known for rust, and can collapse if the car's weight is put on them.

point in the bodywork for the Panhard rod or radius arm mountings (dependent on model), and, just as importantly, the area of anchorage of the rear springs into the bodywork on the non-IRS cars.

While underneath the car, check the exhaust system for leaks and, also, for damage (these cars sit quite low to the ground), and for poor fitting and rattles. A single pipe system was used on the 2.4-litre Mark 1 and

Rear underside looking back, showing the shock absorber mounting and the leaf springs that are mounted inside the bodywork on the non-independent rear suspension cars.

A stainless steel exhaust system is an advantage. This is the underside looking forward, the bulge on the right is the spare wheel well, and on the left, the fuel tank of all models except S-types/420s.

Mark 2, with twin pipes running together on the 3.4- and 3.8-litre models and later 240/340s. For the Daimlers, S-types, and 420s, a twin pipe system ran each side of the floorpan, exiting at each rear corner. Check the fuel tank(s): on the Mark 1, Mark 2, 240/340, and Daimler models this is a single tank mounted beneath the boot floor, and quite prone to corrosion because of its position. The S-types and 420s have two fuel tanks, so ensure they're both checked. Also, check the condition of all the fuel lines and brake lines, the latter are often neglected until they fail an MoT.

Lastly, and on the assumption that you've already test driven the car, look underneath where you parked the car and check for fluid leaks that you might not have noticed – coolant, engine oil, transmission fluid, rear axle oil, even fuel.

Interior

④ ③ ② ①

All these models feature a combination of wood trim, vinyl, and leather or Ambla seat coverings. The first test is to smell the interior – is it musty, indicating dampness? A poor sign.

Start your intensive look at the interior with the woodwork, the majority of which is veneered onto a softwood base. There's a lot of woodwork in these cars and it can be expensive to refurbish or replace. Over time, some areas are affected by bleaching from sunlight, dulling the finish, and, in severe cases even cracking veneer, and the same can occur

A restored S-type interior, though not to original condition; the soft furnishing are too light, the woodwork is too dark, and the carpets the wrong colour.

A very original Mark 2 interior (note the lack of centre woodwork compared to the S-type/420 models). The steering wheel is a period Derrington extra.

A completely original Mark 1 interior with rare split-bench seating and automatic transmission.

A very presentable complete 420 interior, but with faded soft trim, badly soiled carpets, and some cracking of the wood veneer.

through water ingress. The worst affected area is usually the dashboard top rail (this is part-Ambla covered on the 420 models, and on some of the very late Daimler V8s and a few 240 models). The door capping tops also suffer badly from water damage and fading, although these are stained rather than veneered. All repairs to the woodwork, particularly where veneer is concerned, can be very expensive to put right and working on a single panel repair may work, but it's doubtful a good match will be achieved to the rest of the trim. The situation is compounded with the earlier Mark 1 models that have complex wooden surrounds to each door window. These can be difficult to remove for repair, and impossible to replace without having new sets made up at great expense. The S-types and 420s have extra wood veneered panels around the centre instrument/switch cluster, and on the centre console.

Next, check the condition of the headlining and sun visors which, although acceptable if a little grubby, should still be intact, undamaged, and well stretched. On the very early examples of the Mark 2 models, the sun visors were made of stiffened board and were set into the headlining. Over time, the clips fail and the boards bend, preventing them from sitting properly. Replacement boards would have to be made. Some cars assembled abroad (known as CKD – complete knocked down kits), had an element of local input. These cars had a cheaper, vinyl headlining that is worthless today.

Door, kick board, and armrests are vinyl, and usually discolour and harden with age.

All door trims were produced in vinyl (never leather), attached to boards that eventually deteriorate through ingress of damp, the signs of which are warping, with wrinkling and discolouring of the material. The attached armrests are also damaged easily, and, if water had taken a hold, the map pockets can be sodden, with the material breaking away. Vinyl and Rexine was used for other areas of trim, like the kick panels in the front footwells, the centre consoles, and the under-dash liners; these are less prone to problems, although the latter may be completely missing in some cases.

All UK models, except for the 240 and 340, had original equipment leather-faced seating, although some may have been specially ordered with leather or changed by later owners. Only the seat facings are leather, the sides being vinyl as a cost saving exercise. 240/340s and a few Mark 2 and S-types had Ambla upholstery (imitation leather) that wears quite well,

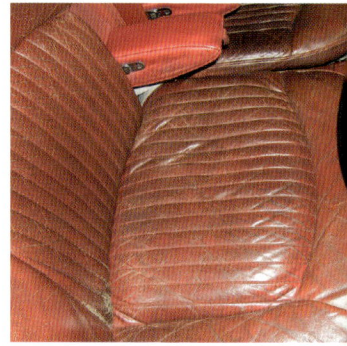

With leather seating, look for bad cracks and tears. More general wear and tear like this is repairable.

but can discolour and split with age, but it is significantly cheaper to replace than leather. Again, some cars assembled in hot climate areas during the 1960s, were also locally equipped with plastic or vinyl upholstery, not to the standard of the British-assembled cars.

The seating styles of the Mark 1, Mark 2, 240/340, S-types, and 420s are all different. Only the Mark 2 featured occasional tables fitted into the back of the front seats, with wood finished facings. These were never fitted to any of the other models. A rarity with the Mark 2, but an extra cost option, was the fitting of front seat reclining mechanisms: now very hard to come by and commanding a premium on the price of a car being sold with them. These were standard on S-types and 420s.

Check all the seating for tears, major cracks in the leather, previous repairs, deteriorating stitching, and sagging of the cushions, all of which can be addressed, albeit at further cost. Complete re-upholstery kits are available but, particularly in leather, are very expensive.

All these cars had fitted carpets with leatherbound edges, underfelt, and anti-drum material. Carpets are held in place by special fasteners, and the older carpets are prone to curling at the edges. Obvious heavy wear areas are the heel pads in the front footwells. Replacement carpets are not that expensive so, dependent on the price of the car, there's little reason why they shouldn't have been replaced. However, a new set of carpets can hide problems with the floor underneath, so lift them to check.

From the introduction of the Mark 2, all these models have the same instrument layout, with minor differences in calibration according to model and year of production, and the same toggle switches. Speedometer cables are prone to weakening, causing the mph needle to flutter considerably. The clock, mounted on the centre top of the dashboard in the 420s, and inset into the rev counter on all other models, hardly ever works, although modern 'innards' are available. Very early Mark 2s featured a different 100psi oil pressure gauge; this was soon changed to read a maximum of 60psi, so that normal readings didn't look low. As the S-types and 420s are equipped with twin fuel tanks, a fuel tank change-over switch on the dashboard replaced one of the interior light switches.

Mark 1 models have an entirely different dashboard, instrument, and switch layout. Speedometers suffer the same problem as the other models, and the oil pressure gauge is directly fed from an oil feed from the engine. If this gauge doesn't work or behaves erratically, this should be investigated as this type of gauge gives a far more accurate account of engine oil pressure than the later types.

The centre console area of the Mark 2 showing the basic heater control slides and the scuttle vent lever.

Under the centre dashboard area there's a handle to operate the scuttle ventilator for the heating system. Ensure this operates because it's prone to seizure or, if broken, won't remain in the open position. This is an ideal opportunity to check the heating and ventilation system, which isn't very efficient! The very simple controls include either a lever on the dashboard (Mark 1 models), chromed knobs on the S-type/420s, or slider controls on the centre console of the other cars. Very basic, they merely control the temperature and direction of air via cables: these often seize or are incorrectly adjusted so they don't operate correctly. The fan is controlled by a dash-mounted switch. The heating systems are notoriously poor, but if totally ineffective and the controls are working correctly, this could be down to furring in the water pipes that run across the bulkhead in the engine compartment. They're small bore and clog easily, the only solution being to dismantle, clean out, or replace. Alternatively, the problem may lie with the heater matrix; this will necessitate stripping the heater box and repairing or replacing the matrix.

Finally, check all the other controls to see if everything works. Interior roof lighting (which varies from model to model), map light, courtesy light switches in the doors, cigarette lighter, audio system, dipping mirror, etc.

Engine bay

Given the checks you made in the fifteen minute evaluation, now look in more detail at areas such as the condition of the inner wings. The normal finish is paint to match the exterior colour scheme, the same applying to the inner bonnet area, although many have now been painted matt black. Corrosion isn't a major issue with either of these areas. Review the fit and condition of the ancillary equipment, like the screen washer bottle, brake and clutch master cylinders, rubbers, pipework, and power steering reservoir (if fitted).

A good, dry engine bay, like this Daimler V8, makes it easier to check for overall condition.

Engine

In addition to your original checks, look at the condition of the engine mountings, particularly the stabiliser mounting on the rear bulkhead. Check the oil feed pipes at the back of the engine to see if they're leaking oil. Look carefully behind the engine and down by the bell-housing for oil leaks, and then look for oil leaks coming from the rear bottom of the engine, signs of a worn or damaged crankshaft rear oil seal (this alone requires the engine to be removed to rectify). There should be no leaks from the crank front oil seal, the timing chest, or the breather housing. The cam covers should seal well without any leaks. Check the sump pan and the sump plug; these shouldn't leak at all. If leaking from the plug itself, it could mean replacing both the plug and the sump pan.

Examine the condition of the core plugs in the block that are visible (you won't be able to see them all), are any seeping coolant? Carefully inspect the cylinder block for cracks, particularly along the top of the block parallel to its face. Are there any signs of coolant seeping elsewhere, like from the water pump or the cylinder head? Is there any play in the cooling fan and are the drive belts in good condition? Does the engine look as if it has recently had work carried out or been steam cleaned? If so, investigate with the owner – what was done and why?

With the engine running, check the running of the crankshaft damper at the front – is it running straight and true, or is there oscillation that could cause excessive strain on the crankshaft? Aftermarket crankshaft dampers aren't that reliable.

It's also worth verifying the engine that is fitted to the car. Is it the original (from the paperwork)? Is it of the correct capacity for that model (affecting Jaguars only)? The cylinder heads of the XK engines are colour coded dependent on model:

Silver   2.4-litre Mark 1 & Mark 2 plus 240/340 and 420
Duck egg blue   3.4-litre Mark 1 & Mark 2 plus S-type

Mid blue   3.8-litre Mark 2 & S-type

Although they may have been changed, the twin-cam rocker box covers also altered according to year of manufacture; polished alloy on all cars up to 1967, thereafter painted black/ribbed covers on all models.

A final confirmation of the engine type fitted can be found from the engine designation, these are:

2.4-litre Mark 1	B
2.4-litre Mark 2	BG onwards
240	7J001 onwards
3.4-litre Mark 1	KE-KF
3.4-litre Mark 2	KG-KH-KJ
340	7J50001 onwards
3.4-litre S-type	7B
3.8-litre Mark 2	LA-LB-LC-LE
3.8-litre S-type	7B
420	7F
420 Sovereign	7A

All Jaguar XK engines have colour-coded cylinder heads.

Cooling system

A more detailed check of the radiator condition doesn't go amiss; look for damage or coolant leaks, and remove the pressure cap to check the condition of the coolant. Coolant should always comprise a good 50/50 mix of the correct blue or green anti-freeze solution, to avoid corrosion of the aluminium cylinder head. These old systems should NEVER be fitted with red anti-freeze.

If the engine is over-heating, even if only slightly, it could be down to the incorrect type of thermostat fitted (often the case). The correct bellows type provides good cooling properties and improves water flow through the heating system.

Fuel system

All the cars covered here have conventional carburettors, twin Solex downdraught on the 2.4-litre models (up to the introduction of the 240), and twin SUs (HD6 1¾in on the Daimlers and all the other XK engine cars, except the 420 which used HD8 2in SUs).

The Solex carburettors are the most basic and least efficient, and have always caused minor issues with over-fuelling when hot, but are generally trouble free. 2.4s and Daimlers had a manual choke system operated by a lever on the driver's side of the dashboard, all others used an automated enrichment device. Some owners fitted a manual cut-off to prevent these devices over-fuelling the car when not cutting off soon enough after warm-up. The SU carburettors are very reliable and servicing kits are readily available. Check that the throttle linkage to the accelerator works smoothly and allows the correct amount of movement, and look for any fuel leaks from banjo connections and pipework. A single bowl-type fuel filter is affixed to the inner wing on the inlet side, and should be clean and carry a paper filter to collect any debris. Single fuel pumps are situated in the boot (nearside) on all models, except for the S-types and 420s with twin tanks, which have one pump per side.

In the majority of cases it's a simple matter to check the condition of the air filter, which will give a good indication of regular maintenance. Disregarding the

Mark 1 and very early Mark 2 which have a complex oil bath air cleaner arrangement, all the other models use a conventional paper element that is easy to inspect. Mark 2 had a large pancake filter situated on top of the engine; a single wing nut allows the cover to be removed. Early Daimler 2.5s also have one pancake; later (250s) have twin filters, and the 240/340s, S-types, and 420s have an oval housing with clips.

All 2.4- and 3.8-litre Mark 2s had this single pancake air filter arrangement.

Electrics

Some of these cars may still be operating on a positive earthing system, so beware if needing to connect a battery charger or jump leads to the car. Although the more modern negative earthing system is far better, positive earthing presents no real detriment and it can easily be changed later if required. Does the battery look in good condition and, more importantly, is it of sufficient size and power for a Jaguar? Around 300 amperes is required, but all too often people fit cheap batteries that can't cope with the power required.

An obviously small battery improperly secured is indicative of poor maintenance. Corrosion of the bulkhead behind the battery is another common problem, caused by leaking batteries.

Look at the general state of the wiring, where practical, and the control box. Any re-wiring is an expensive job, particularly for the time taken to remove and fit a new loom. Check the condition of the plug leads, and remove the distributor cap to check on the condition of the points and rotor arm. The distributor bob weights should be free and snap back under spring tension when released. Many aftermarket rotor arms are unreliable so it's worth checking the condition. Some owners may have fitted electronic ignition, so although there isn't a lot to check here, do look for a tidy and neat installation.

Most of these cars were equipped with a conventional dynamo as standard (except for models like the V8-250) but many may have been changed for an alternator, which is of no detriment. Whatever is fitted, does it look in good condition and is it charging the battery? If an alternator has been installed, the original ammeter (if still wired in) won't accept the output from an alternator, so it will only show a discharge, not a charge rate.

The twin-tone horns are fitted in a vulnerable position (underneath the front of the car) and collect a lot of debris from the road, corroding badly. Ensure they work, and is the wiring intact and undamaged? A single-tone horn can lead to an MoT failure! On post-1964 cars, a different style of steering wheel was used (with a gold growler badge in the centre instead of red), allowing the horns to be operated either from the half-horn ring or a centre push button – do they both operate the horns?

The front side lights of Mark 2, 240/340s, and Daimlers dim badly over the years due to ingress of damp and corrosion in the wing 'pod.' The headlights were never very efficient, particularly the flat glass type fitted to early Mark 2s. The wiring connections can corrode and the silvered reflectors degrade. The same scenario applies to the spot/fog lights, but all the lights are readily available for replacement.

Transmission

All cars were fitted with a four-speed manual transmission, with or without overdrive on top gear. Until 1964, this had no synchromesh on first gear, giving a long throw from 1st to 2nd and a degree of transmission noise noticeable in 1st, which is normal. The synchromesh is relatively slow and the gearbox can take a bit of getting used to, but it's hard wearing and gives very little trouble. In 1964, an all-synchromesh gearbox was introduced on the S-type, a year later on the Mark 2, and was always fitted to the 240/340 and 420/Sovereign. Although still a little 'stodgy,' these 'boxes have a strong synchromesh. The overdrive unit is of contemporary Laycock design, operated electrically by a steering column mounted stalk on all models except the Mark 1, where a dashboard mounted switch was used. Overdrive operation 'in' and 'out' should be smooth, dependent on pedal pressure, and the only common problems are electrical switch failures or with the operating solenoid attached to the overdrive unit.

Check the overdrive is working correctly; it is operated via a steering column-mounted stalk or dash-mounted switch.

The hydraulic clutches are relatively heavy, but acceptable, and should release fully every time without problem. With the introduction of the all synchromesh gearbox, a 9½in diaphragm clutch was used for lighter operation. It's common to find the master cylinder leaking from old seals, so it's worth checking the fluid level and condition. If a clutch is slipping or juddering badly, consider that it's necessary to remove the engine to fit a new clutch.

Automatic transmission was available from 1957 until the end of production, always a Borg Warner three-speed unit, the DG version fitted with a unique feature, the Intermediate Speed Hold. This was a dashboard mounted switch enabling a gear to be held regardless of throttle. The Type DG gearbox was used on most Jaguar models up to the introduction of the 240/340, when the unit was changed to the Model 35, the same transmission as used in the Daimler V8 models (and some later Mark 2s). From 1965, the transmission was modified to provide the D1 and D2 positions, to give the driver the option of a 2nd gear start. The two 420 models used the Model 8 transmission, also offering a D1 and D2 position. None of these transmissions can be compared with modern day automatics, so will not be as smooth or provide the same amount of torque at the wheels. However, they're very strong units and will work for years without trouble (apart from a few oil leaks). Areas of concern are very poor gear changes, which can be put down to adjustment of the bands, or the 'box in need of an oil and filter change. Checking the transmission fluid was covered in the fifteen minute evaluation, but any strong burnt smell or dark colour can signify problems ahead.

The rear axle gives very little trouble and the differentials are long lived. 3.8-litre models normally came with a Powr-Lok differential to aid traction. To check whether this is fitted and working requires the rear of the car to be jacked so that both wheels are off the ground. With the car out of gear and the handbrake off, turn one of the rear wheels by hand; the opposite wheel should turn in the same direction.

Brakes

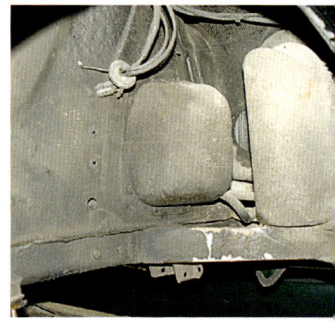

Very early Mark 1s aside, all these cars are equipped with Dunlop all-round disc brakes. Until early in 1959, disc braked cars had round pads that necessitated stripping down the cylinders to change them. In 1959 these were changed for the more common square pads, enabling them to be changed without dismantling. Cars equipped with wire wheels make it relatively easy to check the condition of items like the discs, otherwise it's necessary to remove the road wheels to inspect them properly.

You're looking for the condition of the discs; badly scored, wearing thin, badly corroded around the outer edges, or even cracked. Look at the condition of the brake calipers, which often corrode badly, and inspect the brake pads for wear. Review the brake hoses for condition, connections, and look for leaks, which should be easy to identify.

All models are fitted with a brake servo, sited inside the front driver's side wing area, behind a shield; on the 420/Sovereign this was on the opposite side. The

The brake servo on all cars except the 420 is secured in the front driver's side wing area, with its vacuum storage tank alongside; both with shields that corrode quite badly because of their location.

shield can corrode or be missing entirely – a bad sign! Check the condition of the brake master cylinder, and the fluid level and condition inside; it should be clean. Any loss of fluid could mean fluid is finding its way into the servo, requiring a re-seal at the very least. A vital part of the car's operational system, it's quite easy to identify if everything is in good condition and regularly serviced. The brake system is very good, and quite capable of meeting today's demanding road conditions, but there are many upgrades now available which also work very well. One of the common changes is to fit the discs, calipers, and uprights from a 420 to a Mark 2.

Drum brakes were only fitted to the early 2.4- and 3.4-litre Mark 1, and were a pretty simple installation designed by Lockheed. They're not prone to problems, although, inevitably, some brake fade can be experienced with constant hard use (which is why disc brakes came to the fore). As the drum system requires the use of linings instead of pads, replacements aren't always available off the shelf, so an exchange basis is organised, exchanging your old shoes for re-lined replacements.

Steering

All these cars feature a Burman re-circulating ball steering box system, requiring little maintenance. Some sloppiness in the system may be down to the steering box needing a rebuild. The pin and bush can wear quickly on the diver's side, so later nylon bushes are a better bet. Power assistance was available as an optional extra from the introduction of the Mark 2, but only for the larger engine models, and an improved Adwest system was adopted (again, as an optional extra) for the later Mark 2, 340, 420, and V8-250 models. 2.4s and 240s were never fitted with power-assisted steering. Other than switching on the engine and turning the wheel from lock to lock to identify any unnecessary noises or 'feel' through the wheel, checking the fluid condition and smell in the reservoir, the filer, and looking at the unions and connections, is about all one can do within the realms of this evaluation.

Suspension

The front suspension is mounted on a separate subframe, attached to the main structure of the body, but insulated by Metalastic bonded rubber mountings. These

mountings can eventually fail, indicated by knocking noises from the front of the car: a relatively easy inspection underneath can identify the problem. The front suspension is of the semi-trailing wishbone type, with large coil springs into which the shock absorbers are fitted. Shock absorber wear can be easily identified by pushing down on the front of the car, checking for rebound. The springs can wear reducing the ride height,

Restored front suspension arrangement of the Mark 1 and Mark 2 models.

and individual coils can break. Changing the springs must be done with proper equipment, a cheap High Street spring compressor is of no use! Other items to check are the condition of the torque arms, and ball joints.

At the rear, there are two totally different systems used on these models. The Mark 1, Mark 2, 240/340, and Daimlers all used conventional cantilevered leaf springs, housed at the front within the longitudinal box sections of the monocoque, and attached at the rear by rubber mountings. Telescopic shock absorbers are used, secured to the rear axle at their base, and to the rear bodyshell, accessed from inside the boot. Check the condition of the rubber mountings and the condition of the leaf springs, as leaves often break. There's also a single Panhard rod connecting the rear axle to the bodywork on the offside, and is prone to premature failure. If breaks, it makes an alarming knocking sound.

The rear suspension on the S-types and 420s forms the basis of a complete independent unit, housed within a removable cage, the original design conceived for the larger MkX saloon and the E-type sports car. The cage contains the differential

Good to have a full tool kit, handbooks, workshop manual – and even a period brochure – with the car.

and all the suspension components, attached to the body via Metalastic mountings and radius arms, one per side. Check the mountings for condition, and the fore and aft mountings for the radius arms. The arms themselves corrode badly, as does the bodywork where they connect. Check the condition of the universal joints by pushing in at the top of the wheels. Also check the wheel bearings by rocking the wheels from side to side; only slight play should be felt. There are four shock absorbers, two per side, that can be checked in the same way as the front. The rear disc brakes are mounted in-board either side of the differential, so are difficult to access; the pads are easy to change, but the discs are not. Look for signs of regular and proper maintenance here. The handbrake mechanism and pads are also centrally mounted, and are extremely difficult to access for proper adjustment. If the differential has been leaking at any time, this will show deposits of oil splattered onto the discs and calipers. It's also important to check for play at the inner and outer fulcrum points, and a tyre lever and some judicious prying will reveal any serious wear. Look for good signs of maintenance, like grease on the nipples.

Other areas to check

Don't forget the boot area. All these cars had a simple Hardura matting in the boot. Is it in good condition? All the cars had a comprehensive tool kit, fitted inside the spare wheel under the boot floor; a metal box on most, plastic on the 240, 340, 420, and 250. Is it still there and, if so, is it complete?

Does the car have any of its original paperwork, like the handbook, service book, Jaguar dealership listing booklet, and the wallet they all fitted in?

Evaluation procedure

Add up the total points score: 68 = perfect; 51 = good; 34 = average; 17 = buyer beware! Cars scoring over 48 should be completely usable and require the minimum of repair or rectification, although continued service maintenance and care will be required to keep them in good condition. Cars scoring between 17 and 35 will require serious work (at much the same cost regardless of score). Cars scoring between 36 and 47 will require very careful assessment of the necessary repair costs in order to reach a realistic resale value.

10 Auctions

– sold! Another way to buy your dream

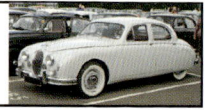

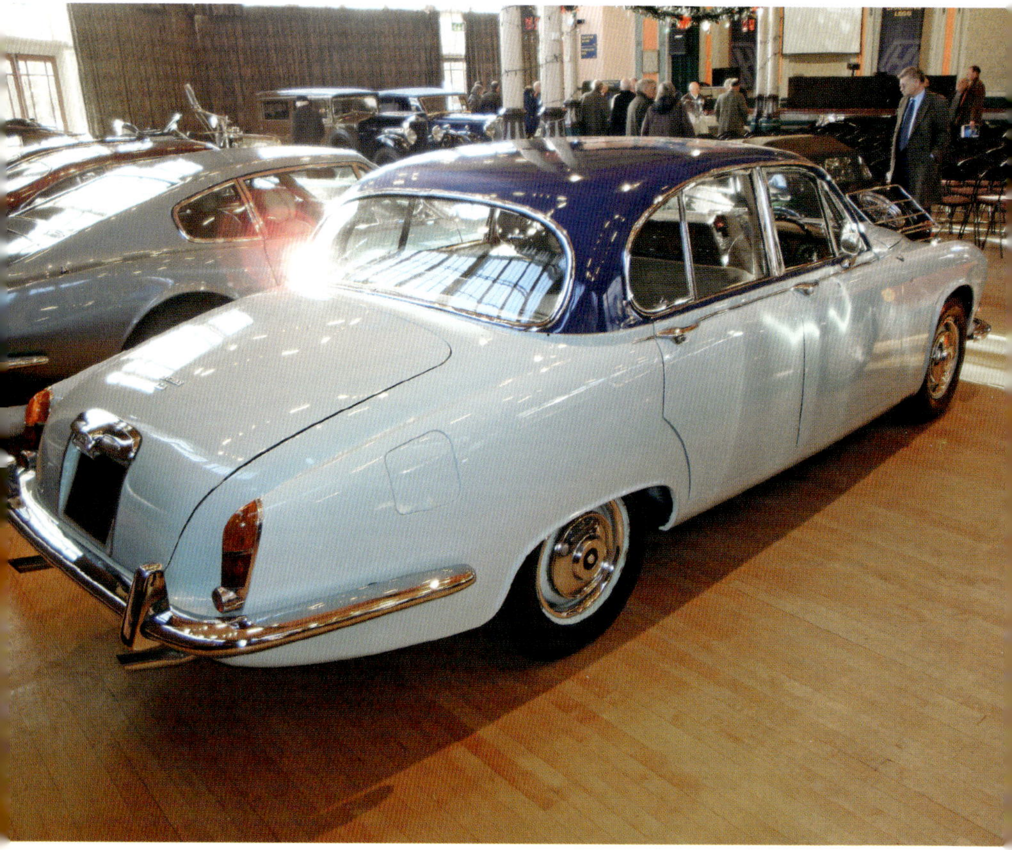

Bargains and unusual cars can be found at auction, like this ex-Lord Mountbatten 420.

Auction pros & cons

Pros: Prices are usually lower than those of dealers or private sellers and you might grab a real bargain on the day. Auctioneers have usually established clear title with the seller. At the venue you can usually examine documentation relating to the vehicle.

Cons: You have to rely on a sketchy catalogue description of condition and history. The opportunity to inspect is limited and you cannot drive the car. Auction cars are often a little below par and may require some work. It's easy to overbid. There will usually be a buyer's premium to pay in addition to the auction hammer price.

Which auction?

Auctions by established auctioneers are advertised in car magazines and on the auction houses' websites. A catalogue, or a simple printed list of the lots for auctions might only be available a day or two ahead, though often lots are listed and pictured on auctioneers' websites much earlier. Contact the auction company to ask if previous auction selling prices are available as this is useful information (details of past sales are often available on websites).

Catalogue, entry fee and payment details

When you purchase the catalogue of the vehicles in the auction, it often acts as a ticket allowing two people to attend the viewing days and the auction. Catalogue details tend to be comparatively brief, but will include information such as 'one owner from new, low mileage, full service history,' etc. It will also usually show a guide price to give you some idea of what to expect to pay and will tell you what is charged as a 'Buyer's premium.' The catalogue will also contain details of acceptable forms of payment. At the fall of the hammer an immediate deposit is usually required, the balance payable within 24 hours. If the plan is to pay by cash there may be a cash limit. Some auctions will accept payment by debit card. Sometimes credit or charge cards are acceptable, but will often incur an extra charge. A bank draft or bank transfer will have to be arranged in advance with your own bank as well as with the auction house. No car will be released before all payments are cleared. If delays occur in payment transfers then storage costs can accrue.

Buyer's premium

A buyer's premium will be added to the hammer price: don't forget this in your calculations. It is not usual for there to be a further state tax or local tax on the purchase price and/or on the buyer's premium.

Viewing

In some instances it's possible to view on the day, or days before, as well as in the hours prior to, the auction. There are auction officials available who are willing to help out by opening engine and luggage compartments and to allow you to inspect the interior. While the officials may start the engine for you, a test drive is out of the question. Crawling under and around the car as much as you want is permitted, but you can't suggest that the car you are interested in be jacked up, or attempt to do the job yourself. You can also ask to see any documentation available.

Bidding

Before you take part in the auction, decide your maximum bid – and stick to it!

It may take a while for the auctioneer to reach the lot you are interested in, so use that time to observe how other bidders behave. When it's the turn of your car, attract the auctioneer's attention and make an early bid. The auctioneer will then look to you for a reaction every time another bid is made, usually the bids will be in fixed increments until the bidding slows, when smaller increments will often be accepted before the hammer falls. If you want to withdraw from the bidding, make sure the auctioneer understands your intentions – a vigorous shake of the head when he or she looks to you for the next bid should do the trick!

Assuming that you are the successful bidder, the auctioneer will note your card or paddle number, and from that moment on you will be responsible for the vehicle.

If the car is unsold, either because it failed to reach the reserve or because there was little interest, it may be possible to negotiate with the owner, via the auctioneers, after the sale is over.

Successful bid
There are two more items to think about. How to get the car home, and insurance. If you can't drive the car, your own or a hired trailer is one way, another is to have the vehicle shipped using the facilities of a local company. The auction house will also have details of companies specialising in the transfer of cars.

Insurance for immediate cover can usually be purchased on site, but it may be more cost-effective to make arrangements with your own insurance company in advance, and then call to confirm the full details.

eBay & other online auctions
eBay and other online auctions could land you a car at a bargain price, though you'd be foolhardy to bid without examining the car first, something most vendors encourage. A useful feature of eBay is that the geographical location of the car is shown, so you can narrow your choices to those within a realistic radius of home. Be prepared to be outbid in the last few moments of the auction. Remember, your bid is binding and that it will be very, very difficult to get restitution in the case of a crooked vendor fleecing you – caveat emptor!

Be aware that some cars offered for sale in online auctions are 'ghost' cars. Don't part with any cash without being sure that the vehicle does actually exist and is as described (usually pre-bidding inspection is possible).

Auctioneers
Barrett-Jackson: www.barrett-jackson.com
Bonhams: www.bonhams.com
British Car Auctions (BCA): www.bca-europe.com or www.british-car-auctions.co.uk
Cheffins: www.cheffins.co.uk
Christies: www.christies.com
Coys: www.coys.co.uk
eBay: www.eBay.com
H&H: www.classic-auctions.co.uk
RM: www.rmauctions.com
Shannons: www.shannons.com.au
Silver: www.silverauctions.com

11 Paperwork
– correct documentation is essential!

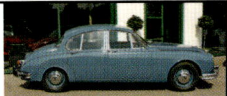

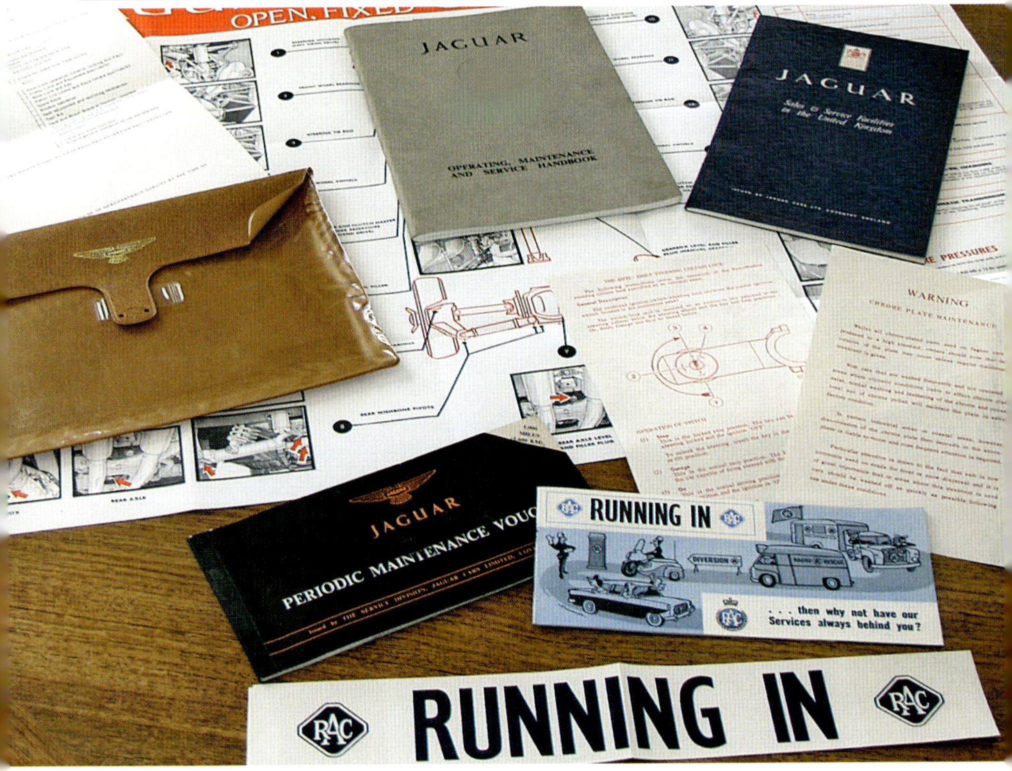

The more history you get with the car the better.

Classic, collector and prestige cars usually come with a large portfolio of paperwork accumulated and passed on by a succession of proud owners. This documentation represents the real history of the car and from it can be deduced the level of care the car has received, how much it's been used, which specialists have worked on it and the dates of major repairs and restorations. All of this information will be priceless to you as the new owner, so be very wary of cars with little paperwork to support their claimed history.

Registration documents

All countries/states have some form of registration for private vehicles whether it's like the American 'pink slip' system or the British 'log book' system.

It is essential to check that the registration document is genuine, that it relates to the car in question, and that all the vehicle's details are correctly recorded, including chassis/VIN and engine numbers (if these are shown). If you are buying from the previous owner, his or her name and address will be recorded in the document: this will not be the case if you are buying from a dealer.

In the UK the current (Euro-aligned) registration document is named V5C, and is printed in coloured sections of blue, green and pink. The blue section relates to the car specification, the green section has details of the new owner and the pink section is sent to the DVLA in the UK when the car is sold. A small section in yellow deals with selling the car within the motor trade.

In the UK the DVLA will provide details of earlier keepers of the vehicle upon payment of a small fee, and much can be learned in this way.

If the car has a foreign registration there may be expensive and time-consuming formalities to complete. Do you really want the hassle?

Roadworthiness certificate

Most country/state administrations require that vehicles are regularly tested to prove that they are safe to use on the public highway and do not produce excessive emissions. In the UK that test (the 'MoT') is carried out at approved testing stations, for a fee. In the USA the requirement varies, but most states insist on an emissions test every two years as a minimum, while the police are charged with pulling over unsafe-looking vehicles.

In the UK the test is required on an annual basis once a vehicle becomes three years old. Of particular relevance for older cars is that the certificate issued includes the mileage reading recorded at the test date and, therefore, becomes an independent record of that car's history. Ask the seller if previous certificates are available. Without an MoT the vehicle should be trailored to its new home, unless you insist that a valid MoT is part of the deal. (Not such a bad idea this, as at least you will know the car was roadworthy on the day it was tested and you don't need to wait for the old certificate to expire before having the test done.)

Road licence

The administration of every country/state charges some kind of tax for the use of its road system, the actual form of the 'road licence,' and how it is displayed, varying enormously country to country and state to state.

Whatever the form of the 'road licence,' it must relate to the vehicle carrying it and must be present and valid if the car is to be driven on the public highway legally. The value of the license will depend on the length of time it will continue to be valid.

In the UK if a car is untaxed because it has not been used for a period of time, the owner has to inform the licensing authorities, otherwise the vehicle's date-related registration number will be lost and there will be a painful amount of paperwork to get it re-registered.

Also, in the UK, vehicles built before the end of 1972 are provided with 'tax discs' free of charge, but they must still display a valid disc. Car clubs can often provide formal proof that a particular car qualifies for this valuable concession.

Certificates of authenticity

For many makes of collectible car it is possible to get a certificate proving the age and authenticity (eg: engine and VIN/chassis numbers, paint colour and trim) of a particular vehicle, these are called 'Heritage Certificates,' and if the car comes with one of these it is a definite bonus. If you want to obtain one for one of these models, apply to Jaguar Heritage in Coventry, England.

If the car has been used in European classic car rallies, it may have a FIVA (Federation Internationale des Vehicules Anciens) certificate. The so-called 'FIVA Passport', or 'FIVA Vehicle Identity Card,' enables organisers and participants to recognise whether or not a particular vehicle is suitable for individual events. If you want to obtain such a certificate go to www.fbhvc.co.uk or www.fiva.org; there will be similar organisations in other countries too.

Valuation certificate

Hopefully, the vendor will have a recent valuation certificate, or letter signed by a recognised expert stating how much he, or she, believes the particular car to be worth (such documents, together with photos, are usually needed to get 'agreed value' insurance). Generally such documents should act only as confirmation of your own assessment of the car rather than a guarantee of value as the expert has probably not seen the car in the flesh. The easiest way to find out how to obtain a formal valuation is to contact the owners' club.

Service history

Often, older cars will have been serviced at home by enthusiastic (and hopefully capable) owners for a good number of years. Nevertheless, try to obtain as much service history and other paperwork pertaining to the car as you can. Naturally, dealer stamps, or specialist garage receipts score most points in the value stakes. However, anything helps in the great authenticity game, items like the original bill of sale, handbook, parts invoices and repair bills, adding to the story and the character of the car. Even a brochure correct to the year of the car's manufacture is a useful document, and something that you could well have to search hard to locate in future years. If the seller claims that the car has been restored, then expect receipts and other evidence from a specialist restorer.

If the seller claims to have carried out regular servicing, ask what work was completed, when, and seek some evidence of it being carried out. Your assessment of the car's overall condition should tell you whether the seller's claims are genuine.

Restoration photographs

If the seller tells you that the car has been restored, then expect to be shown a series of photographs taken while the restoration was under way. Pictures taken at various stages, and from various angles, should help you gauge the thoroughness of the work. If you buy the car, ask if you can have all the photographs, as they form an important part of the vehicle's history. It's surprising how many sellers are happy to part with their car and accept your cash, but want to hang on to their photographs! In the latter event, you may be able to persuade the vendor to get a set of copies made.

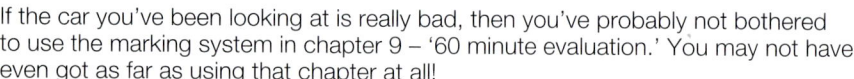

12 What's it worth?
– let your head rule your heart

Condition

If the car you've been looking at is really bad, then you've probably not bothered to use the marking system in chapter 9 – '60 minute evaluation.' You may not have even got as far as using that chapter at all!

If you did use the marking system in chapter 9, you'll know whether the car is in Excellent (maybe Concours), Good, Average or Buyer Beware condition or, perhaps, somewhere in-between these categories.

Many car magazines run a regular price guide. If you haven't bought the latest issues, do so now and compare their suggested values for the model you are thinking of buying: also look at the auction prices they're reporting. Some models will always be more sought-after than others. Trends can change too. The published values tend to vary from one magazine to another, as do the scales of condition, so read the guidance notes carefully. Bear in mind that a car that is in truly magnificent condition or even a recent show winner, could be worth more than the highest scale published. Assuming the car you have in mind is not in show/Concours condition, then relate the level of condition that you judge the car to be in with the appropriate guide price. How does the figure compare with the asking price? Before you start haggling with the seller, consider what affect any variation from standard specification might have on the car's value.

If you are buying from a dealer, remember there will be a dealer's premium on the price.

Desirable options/extras

Just as beauty is in the eye of the beholder, so it is with extras and modifications. Certain extra-cost options when the cars were new are just as desirable now as they were when the owner paid for them. Some later modifications may also be desirable to someone who is using a car regularly, but not to someone who shows their car at events.

Wire wheels are a desirable option on any of these cars; this a 420 model.

Unless to special order, all these models were sold with conventional steel wheels displaying hub caps and, sometimes, rimbellishers. Any model with wire wheels is, therefore, usually considered to be desirable. The finish of these wheels is also personal choice, but chrome costs more and, therefore, may be more desirable to some, albeit more difficult to clean! Some of the very late models, or those re-imported from overseas, may have 'easy clean' wire wheels with non-eared hub spinners. Most prefer the older 'curly' hub types with eared spinners. There are also more modern and expensive wire wheels, like Borrani – highly desirable if fitted, but expensive to repair.

There are very few cosmetic changes made to the cars. Some owners of the later 240/340s have replaced the thin bumpers for the ribbed type from the earlier cars, and, along with spot/fog lights where not previously fitted, this could be considered desirable.

Modern electronic ignition systems are a popular upgrade and make for a more

reliable car. The fitting of thermostatically controlled electric cooling fans is also popular and helps to keep the engines cool, particularly in hot weather. The fitting of a more modern automatic or five-speed manual transmission is much more expensive, but worthwhile if you use the car for touring and aren't bothered about originality. If not wanting to go that far, the earlier (pre-1964) cars do benefit from the fitting of the Jaguar all-synchromesh gearbox, but these are getting more difficult to find.

On the exhaust side, a stainless steel system is advantageous, and owners of the single pipe 2.4-litre cars also benefit from fitting a twin-pipe system. The exhaust manifolds can be upgraded with a multi-branch system, improving gas flow. Stiffer springs be purchased, along with Koni adjustable shock absorbers, all of which help improve handling. Dynamo equipped cars benefit from the fitting of a more efficient alternator, and there are a number of modern power steering conversions that, if fitted correctly, take the strain out of slow speed manoeuvring.

Internally, the fitting of leather upholstery to a car that normally had Ambla is very acceptable, as is the fitting of some period extras, like reclining front seats. A lot of owners fit non-Jaguar wood-rim steering wheels, different gear knobs, etc, that are acceptable up to a point: for example, a small diameter, thick leather rimed steering wheel that would be more at home in a Ford Escort, doesn't give the Jaguar any stret-cred at all!

Major interior changes (the fitting of air-conditioning, for example) are bespoke operations, and have little bearing on price when buying or selling.

Major mechanical changes like the fitting of a later engine is a personal decision, and would be less desirable to many buyers.

Undesirable features

As previously mentioned, a car without matching numbers for engine and gearbox is always going to be worth less, but that doesn't mean to say that the car isn't better for it. Certainly a larger capacity engine, a later engine with bigger valves, or even one fitted with triple carburettors (which requires some bodywork and ancillary alterations under the bonnet), can provide better performance. Any other changes from original may reflect in the value, either when you buy the car or when you come to sell it.

On the subject of gearboxes, automatic transmissions are always

A vinyl roof, and cut-away rear spats, etc, won't go down well with all buyers.

Triple carburettors require many other changes, usually including removal of the battery from the engine bay.

less desirable than manuals, and that applies to cars that still carry their BW designation but have had the 'boxes changed to manual. A similar scenario applies to cars converted from left-hand drive to right or vice versa. There'll always be a stigma to the change which will reflect in pricing.

For normal use, extreme performance upgrades don't suit the car, and also affect the price, despite what it may have cost to carry out the conversions. Major changes, like converting the rear end to independent suspension, converting to rack and pinion steering, or fitting a revised manifold with triple Weber carburettors, with wider, perhaps alloy wheels, may look 'mean and purposeful,' but don't bode well with buyers. It goes without saying that any major non-Jaguar components, like engines, make the car worthless in many eyes.

There are lesser issues. For example, replacing the half spats over the rear wheels of the Mark 2, 240/340s, and Daimler V8s, with cut-away 'Coombes' style glass fibre or metal spats, does allow rear wheel removal without hindrance, but isn't to everyone's taste.

Striking a deal

Negotiate on the basis of your condition assessment, mileage, and fault rectification cost. Also take into account the car's specification. Be realistic about the value, but don't be completely intractable: a small compromise on the part of the vendor or buyer will often facilitate a deal at little real cost.

www.velocebooks.com / www.veloce.co.uk
All current books • New book news • Special offers • Gift vouchers

13 Do you really want to restore?
– it'll take longer and cost more than you think

If you have reasonable skills working with motor cars, and the tools and space to do the work, then it may be within your remit to consider the purchase of a car requiring some remedial attention. There are plenty of examples around, but you need to be careful in differentiating such a car from those that will end up needing a total rebuild. If, on the other hand, you have the experience and expertise to do more, then do include cars requiring a complete restoration in your search. However, extreme care should be taken to thoroughly examine any such candidate to ensure you don't take on more than the car's value will ever justify, or even find that the vehicle is actually beyond redemption.

All classic Jaguars are renowned for their restoration costs, and, certainly, if you use professionals to carry out much of the work, think again; the total cost will far outweigh any price you're likely to get for the car in the foreseeable future. A DIY restoration, on the other hand, could take you years to complete, using up your valuable time and space (let alone money). It's so easy to fall into the trap of restoring some items to perfection, and then, as you re-assemble the car, finding out that other items, that you didn't refurbish so well, make the end product look bad, so you could find yourself refurbishing or replacing more and more.

If you want to go down this route, first decide on the type of work you feel you're capable of carrying out.

Just the beginning of a long and expensive restoration, after removing the mechanicals.

Mechanical work may be your forte, but consider that rebuilding a Jaguar XK or Daimler V8 engine is significantly more complex and costly in parts than working on the average four-cylinder overhead valve unit. The independent rear suspension of the S-types and 420s has a considerable number of components, the cost of which can be outrageous. Conversely, body and paintwork is an art in itself, and these bodies are not only complex, but acquiring the smooth and correct finished shape takes an incredible amount of patient work. Then there's the upholstery. The cost of refurbishing wood veneer – of which there is a considerable amount in these cars – and the cost of replacement leather and other trim, bears no comparison to the cost of doing the same in other, cheaper cars.

On the plus side, all the electrics are pretty basic, and the only concern is having to completely re-wire a car. New looms aren't cheap, and it's a complex and long affair to feed one through every orifice of the car, including the sills; not easy in a car that still has all its trim and drive train in position.

Another advantage is that there is so much available for these models, which is still being remanufactured today. Many of the component parts are also fitted to other Jaguar models, and there are very many specialist suppliers. Then there's the availability of used parts: sources are diverse and include the internet, advertisers in the Jaguar club magazines, and – not least – the many hundreds of classified ads that appear as a result of garage clearouts, the stripping down of abandoned projects, etc.

The bottom line, therefore, is to realistically decide on what you can do, how much you're prepared to put into the project, in time and money, and buy the very best car you can afford as the starting point. You'll always under-estimate the time and work it will take, and the cost involved.

The thought of finding a car like this and commencing a full restoration is daunting. Even if the car you want to restore is in better condition than the one above, you'll still need to spend plenty of time searching scrapyards for parts.

www.velocebooks.com / www.veloce.co.uk
All current books • New book news • Special offers • Gift vouchers

14 Paint problems
– bad complexion, including dimples, pimples and bubbles

Paint faults generally occur due to lack of protection and/or maintenance, or to poor preparation prior to a respray or touch-up. Some of the following conditions may be present in the car you're looking at.

Dull paintwork can sometimes be revived, but old, original paint, particularly 1960s metallics, can be beyond remedial work.

Orange peel
This appears as an uneven paint surface, similar to the appearance of the skin of an orange. The fault is caused by the failure of atomized paint droplets to flow into each other when they hit a surface. It's sometimes possible to rub out the effect with proprietary paint cutting/ rubbing compound or very fine grades of abrasive paper. A respray may be necessary in severe cases. Consult a bodywork repairer/paint shop for advice on the particular car.

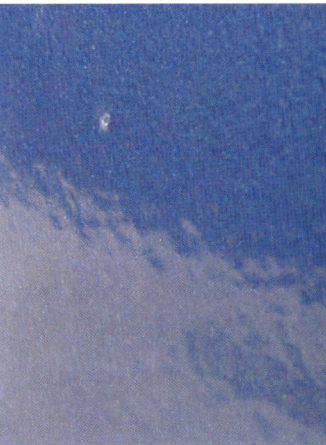

You may be able to rub out orange peel, but in severe cases a respray may be necessary.

Cracking
Severe cases are likely to have been caused by too heavy an application of paint (or filler beneath the paint). Also, insufficient stirring of the paint before application can lead to the components being improperly mixed, and cracking can result. Incompatibility with the paint already on the panel can have a similar effect. To rectify the problem it's necessary to rub down to a smooth, sound finish before respraying the problem area.

Crazing
Sometimes the paint takes on a crazed rather than a cracked appearance when the problems mentioned under 'Cracking' are present. This problem can also be caused by a reaction between the underlying surface and the paint. Paint removal and respraying the problem area is usually the only solution.

When does cracking become crazing? Both will require paint removal and respraying.

Blistering

Almost always caused by corrosion of the metal beneath the paint. Usually perforation will be found in the metal and the damage will usually be worse than that suggested by the area of blistering. The metal will have to be repaired before repainting.

Micro blistering

Usually the result of an economy respray where inadequate heating has allowed moisture to settle on the car before spraying. Consult a paint specialist, but usually damaged paint will have to be removed before partial or full respraying. Can also be caused by car covers that don't 'breathe.'

Blistering is almost always caused by corroded metal beneath the paint.

Fading

Some colours, especially reds, are prone to fading if subjected to strong sunlight for long periods without the benefit of polish protection. Sometimes proprietary paint restorers and/or paint cutting/rubbing compounds will retrieve the situation. Often a respray is the only real solution.

Peeling

Often a problem with metallic paintwork when the sealing lacquer becomes damaged and begins to peel off. Poorly applied paint may also peel. The remedy is to strip and start again!

Dimples

Dimples in the paintwork are caused by the residue of polish (particularly silicone types) not being removed properly before respraying. Paint removal and repainting is the only solution.

Peeling paint occurs when the sealing lacquer becomes damaged: time to strip and start again.

Dents

Small dents are usually easily cured by the 'Dentmaster,' or equivalent process, that sucks or pushes out the dent (as long as the paint surface is still intact). Companies offering dent removal services usually come to your home: consult your telephone directory.

www.velocebooks.com / www.veloce.co.uk
All current books • New book news • Special offers • Gift vouchers

15 Problems due to lack of use

– just like their owners, Jaguar Mark 1s & 2s need exercise!

Cars, like humans, are at their most efficient if they exercise regularly. A run of at least twenty miles, once a week, is recommended for classics.

Seized components
Pistons in calipers, slave and master cylinders can seize.

The clutch may seize if the friction plate becomes stuck to the flywheel because of corrosion.

Handbrakes (parking brakes) can seize if the cables and linkages rust, particularly pertinent with the very early drum braked models.

Pistons can seize in the bores due to corrosion.

Fluids
Old, acidic oil can corrode bearings.

Uninhibited coolant can corrode internal waterways, particularly with the alloy heads of these engines. Lack of the correct mix of antifreeze can cause core plugs to be pushed out, or even cracks in the block or head. Silt settling and solidifying can cause overheating.

Brake fluid absorbs water from the atmosphere and should be renewed every two years. Old fluid with a high water content can cause corrosion and pistons/calipers to seize (freeze), and can cause brake failure when the water turns to vapour near hot braking components.

Tyre problems
Tyres that have had the weight of the car on them in a single position for some time will develop flat spots, resulting in some (usually temporary) vibration. The tyre walls may also have cracks or (blister-type) bulges, meaning new tyres are needed.

People tend to forget that these classics do less mileage than everyday cars, so although tyre wear is not a real factor, the age of the tyres is. Tyres over six years of age are generally considered to be nearing the end of their natural life, regardless of mileage.

Shock absorbers (dampers)
With lack of use, the dampers will lose their elasticity or even seize. Creaking, groaning and stiff suspension are signs of this problem.

Rubber and plastic
Radiator hoses may have perished and split, possibly resulting in the loss of all coolant. Window and door seals can harden and leak. Gaitors/boots can crack. Wiper blades will harden. Metalastic mountings can crack and de-bond.

Electrics
The battery will be of little use if it hasn't been charged for many months. If it leaks, it can cause considerable corrosion around the bulkhead area.

Earthing/grounding problems are common when the connections have corroded. Old bullet and spade type electrical connectors commonly rust/corrode, and will

need disconnecting, cleaning, and protection (eg: Vaseline).
 Sparkplug electrodes will often have corroded in an unused engine.
 Wiring insulation can harden and fail.

Rotting exhaust system
Exhaust gas contains a high water content so exhaust systems corrode very quickly from the inside when the car is not used.

Leaving a car standing in a garage for long periods can have all sorts of disastrous effects on the car's condition; witness, here, corroson and rust to nuts and bolts.

16 The Community

– key people, organisations and companies in the Jaguar Mark 1 & 2 world

Because of the high esteem in which the Jaguar (and Daimler) marques are held, it's not surprising that there is an incredible infrastructure to support them, particularly the classic models from the 1950s and 1960s, like the cars we cover in this publication.

The Jaguar Enthusiasts' Club holds annual technical seminars on specific models.

The Jaguar community is strong and worldwide, with numerous events to enjoy.

Even if you're not well versed in the detail of these particular cars, it won't take you long to become knowledgeable given the tremendous help and support available. Numerous books have been written on the cars, an enormous amount of original literature still survives, and you can still buy original or reprinted copies of workshop and parts manuals. The internet is also a valuable source of information, via any number of sites, bulletin boards, and forums, plus, of course, the Jaguar clubs websites.

There's now a strong network of Jaguar independent specialists who'll maintain these vehicles, carry out refurbishment and restoration, and there are also many well known spares businesses catering for these models. Jaguar Heritage are also involved with a Jaguar Classic Parts Scheme, that can supply some components (although they tend to concentrate on the later neo-classics).

The cars are also very well supported by Jaguar marque clubs, so there's ample opportunity to find out more from existing owners, and seek advice when required. And, finally, there are numerous insurance companies that offer classic and cherished vehicle insurance schemes at very reasonable cost.

Clubs

The Jaguar Drivers Club
18 Stuart Street, Luton, Bedfordshire LU1 2SL
Tel: +44 (0)1582 419 332. www.jaguardriver.co.uk
The oldest of the Jaguar marque clubs, based in the UK, catering for all models with a monthly magazine, insurance scheme, and a good overseas network.

The Jaguar Enthusiasts' Club
Abbeywood Office Park, Emma Chris Way, Filton, Bristol BS34 7JU
Tel: +4 (0)1179 698 186. www.jec.org.uk
   The world's largest Jaguar club, catering for all models with a special Forum
and technical seminars for owners of these models. 132 page full colour monthly
magazine, insurance schemes, technical advice, specialist tools supply and hire plus
events, tours and runs.

Jaguar Clubs of North America
C/o Nelson Rath, 1000 Glenbrook, Anchorage KY 40223
Tel: +1 502 244 1672. www.jcna.com
   The umbrella organisation for the US based Jaguar clubs with an events calendar
and monthly magazine.

The Jaguar Heritage Trust
C/o The Heritage Centre, Browns Lane, Allesley, Coventry CV5 9DR
Tel: +44 (0)2476 401288. www.jdht.com
   Holder of the official Jaguar Cars archive, with information available on car build
details, Heritage Certificate supply, CDs on service/maintenance information, plus
photographic library.

Specialist independent service/maintenance providers
David Marks Garages
Unit 36, Wilford & North Nottingham Industrial Estate, Ruddington Lane, Nottingham
NG11 7EP
Tel: +44 (0)115 982 2808. www.davidmarksgarages.co.uk

R.G Bate (Engineering) Ltd
501 Cleveland Street, Birkenhead, Cheshire CH41 3EF
Tel: +44 (0)151 653 6765

Restorers & restored car sales
Watjag Limited
Great Longstone Business Park, Nr Bakewell, Derbyshire DE45 1TD
Tel: +44 (0)1629 640 776. www.derek-watson.co.uk

JD Classics
Wycke Hill Business Park, Wycke Hill, Maldon, Essex CM9 6UZ
Tel: +44 (0)1621 879 579. www.jdclassics.co.uk

Parts suppliers
SNG Barratt Ltd
Stourbridge Road, Bridgnorth, Shropshire WV15 6AP
Tel: +44 (0)1746 765 432. www.sngbarratt.com

Martin Robey Sales Ltd
Pool Road, Camphill Industrial Estate, Nuneaton, Warwickshire CV10 9AE
Tel: +44 (0)2476 345 302. www.martinrobey.com

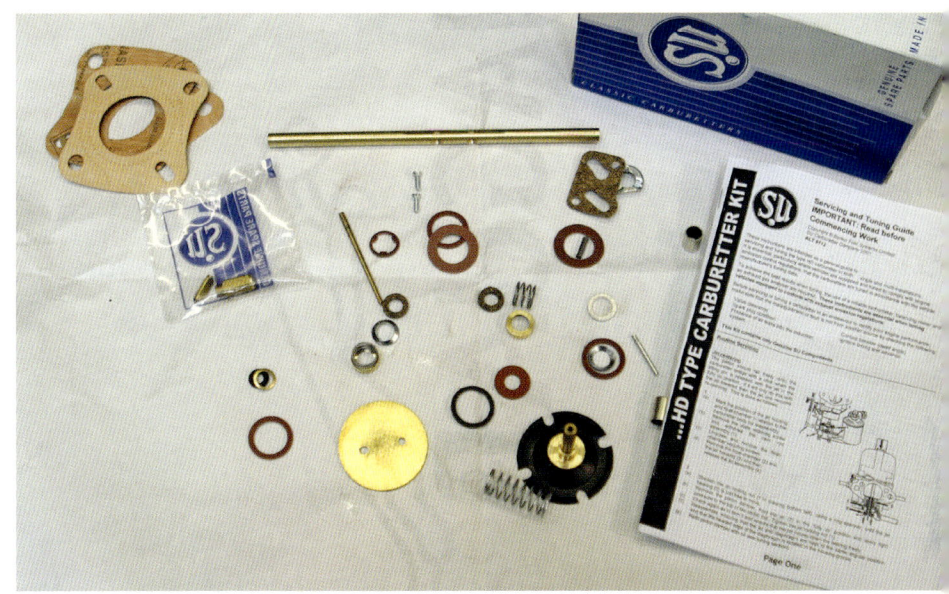

Spares availability is excellent, from new panels to repair kits.

M & C Wilkinson
Everton, Near Doncaster, South Yorkshire
Tel: +44 (0) 1777 818 061. www.jaguar-spares-uk.co.uk

Norman Motors
100 Mill Lane, London NW6 1NF
Tel: +44 (0)20 7431 0940. www.normanmotorsltd.com

Modifications & upgrades
Racing Green Cars
Station Road West, Ashvale, Hampshire GU12 5QD
Tel: +44 (0)1252 544 888. www.racinggreencars.com

BAS International (trim specialists)
10-13 Llantarnam Park Industrial Estate, Cwmbran, South Wales NP44 3AX
Tel: +44 (0)1633 873 664. www.bas-international.com

Zeus Automotive Braking Systems
Unit J2, Dunkeswell Airfield, Honiton, Devon EX14 4LE
Tel: +44 (0)1297 300 010. www.zeus.uk.com

Useful sources of information
Jaguar World Monthly magazine
The independent monthly magazine from Kelsey Publishing, with regular features on
these models.

17 Vital statistics
– essential data at your fingertips

Production figures

2.4-litre Mark 1	19,705	3.8-litre S-type	15,065
3.4-litre Mark 1	17,280	240	4430
2.4-litre Mark 2	26,322	340	2804
3.4-litre Mark 2	29,531	420	10,236
3.8-litre Mark 2	27,848	420 Sovereign	5824
2.5-litre V8	13,018	V8-250	4897
3.4-litre S-type	9928	**Total**	**186,888**

Technical specifications
2.4-litre engine
2483cc six-cylinder dohc 83 x 76.5mm 112bhp @ 5750rpm (133bhp @ 5500rpm, 240) & 140lb/ft @ 2000rpm (146lb/ft @ 3700rpm, 240).
3.4-litre engine
3442cc six-cylinder dohc 83 x 106mm 210bhp @ 5500rpm 216lb/ft @ 3000rpm
3.8-litre engine
3781cc six-cylinder dohc 87 x 106mm 220bhp @ 5500rpm
4.2-litre engine
4235cc six-cylinder dohc 92.07 x 106mm 245bhp @ 5500rpm 283lb/ft @ 3750rpm.
2.5-litre engine
2548cc eight-cylinder 76.2 x 69.85mm 140bhp @ 5800rpm 155lb/ft @ 3600.

Transmissions
4-speed manual gearbox, with or without overdrive on top gear.
Borg Warner 3-speed automatic
2.4-/3.4-litre Mark 1/Mark 2/S-types: DG with intermediate speed hold.
240/340 and Daimler V8s: Model 35
420/Sovereign: Model 8

Dimensions

	Mark 1	Mark 2 & V8	S-type	420/Sovereign
Length	180.75in 4591mm	180.75in 4591mm	187in 4750mm	187.5in 4763mm
Width	66.75in 1695mm	66.75in 1695mm	66.25in 1683mm	67in 1702mm
Height	57.5in 1461mm	57.75in 1467mm	55.75in 1416mm	56.25in 1429mm
Weight	27/28cwt 29.5cwt (3.4)	29.5cwt (3.4) 30cwt (3.8) 29cwt (V8)	32cwt (3.4) 33 cwt (3.8)	33cwt

Suspension
Front: Independent, semi-trailing wishbones, coil springs and anti-roll bars.
Rear: (Mark 1, 2, 240/340 and V8) Live axle, Panhard rod location, and leaf springs.
(S-type/420s) Independent lower wishbone/upper drive shaft link, radius arms, and
coil springs.

Brakes
All-round discs with single calipers. Inboard rear discs on S-types and 420 models,
all with servo assistance.

Steering
Burman recirculating box, some with power assistance.

Wheels
15in (381mm) standard 4J, later $4^1/_2$J and 5J.
Standard steel wheels with option of wire spoked.

Statistics tell you a lot about the performance and fuel consumption of
different models, but you'll still have to decide which model you want – in this
case, a Daimler or a Jaguar.

www.velocebooks.com / www.veloce.co.uk
All current books • New book news • Special offers • Gift vouchers

Also from Veloce Publishing ...

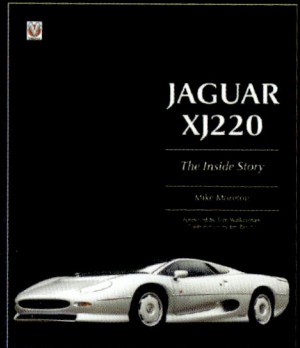

ISBN 978-1-845842-50-5
Hardback • 20.7x25cm
£24.99* UK / $49.95* US
160 pages • 225 pictures

Jaguar XJ220
The Inside Story
Mike Moreton

The Jaguar XJ220 supercar evolved from Jim Randle's sensational 1988 UK Motor Show concept car. The planned production of 350 limited edition cars, each with a price tag of £360,000, was over-subscribed by a factor of four in a single day!

In this book, Mike Moreton, ace director of impossible projects, who was headhunted for the XJ220 project by Tom Walkinshaw, relives the extraordinary inside story of this fantastic, hi-tech car.

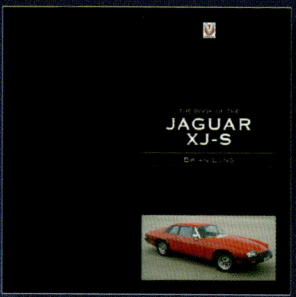

ISBN 978-1-845844-01-1
Hardback • 25x25cm
£30.00* UK / $59.95* US
160 pages • 270 pictures

The book of the
Jaguar XJ-S
Brian Long

New, large format edition of the definitive history of Jaguar's E-type replacement, the XJ-S. More a grand tourer than a sportscar, the controversially styled XJ-S offered a combination of supercar performance and grand tourer luxury.

Not only essential reading, but a great reference source for all owners and would-be owners. Includes really useful advice on buying, running and restoration. Includes 270 photos and illustrations, with rare photos of the prototypes that didn't make production.

*prices subject to change, p&p extra.
For more details visit www.veloce.co.uk or email info@veloce.co.uk

Roads with a View
England's greatest views and how to find them by road
David Corfield

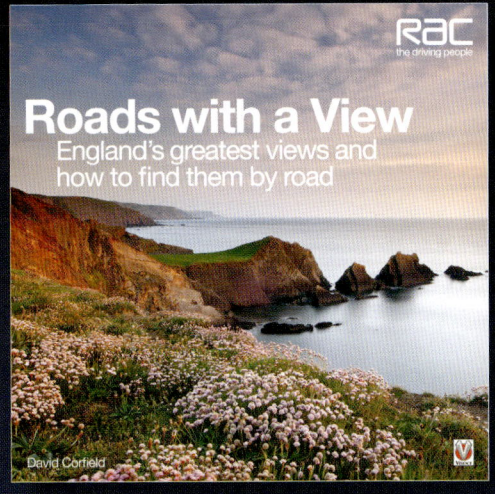

ISBN 978-1-845843-50-2
Hardback • 25x25cm • £19.99* UK / $45* US
• 44 pages • 57 pictures

Roads with a View is not just another travel guide. This one has been written by a driver especially for fellow motorists, and provides detailed accounts of the best roads to drive on, and the best places to drive to for that stunning front seat view. With specially drawn maps, stunningly beautiful colour photography from some of the England's finest landscape photographers, and plenty of travel advice on where to eat, where to stay, and what to do, this unique guide lifts the lid on parts of England that are often overlooked. The author has made sure to include information for everyone – driver as well as passengers – as you seek out England's finest landscapes. With advice on where to stay and where to eat, as well as what to do when you get to the view, this really is an invaluable travel guide.

*prices subject to change, p&p extra.
For more details visit www.veloce.co.uk or email info@veloce.co.uk

The **Essential** Buyer's Guide™ series

 VOLKSWAGEN **BUS** — 978-1-845840-22-8

 TRIUMPH **TR6** — 978-1-845840-26-6

 MG **MGB MGB GT** — 978-1-845840-29-7

JAGUAR **E-type** V12 5.3 litre — 978-1-845840-77-8

CITROËN **2CV** — 978-1-845840-99-0

MORRIS **MINOR & 1000** Saloon, Tourer & Convertible 1952 to 1971 — 978-1-845841-01-0

MERCEDES-BENZ **280-560SL & SLC** 107-series Roadsters & Coupés 1971 to 1989 — 978-1-845841-07-2

MERCEDES-BENZ PAGODA **230, 250 & 280SL** 107-series Roadsters & Coupés 1963 to 1971 — 978-1-845841-13-3

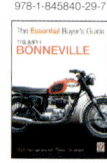 JAGUAR/DAIMLER **XJ6, XJ12 & Sovereign** — 978-1-845841-19-5

TRIUMPH **BONNEVILLE** — 978-1-845841-34-8

BMW **GS** — 978-1-845841-35-5

BSA **500 & 650 Twins** — 978-1-845841-36-2

CITROËN **DS & ID** — 978-1-845841-38-6

ROLLS-ROYCE **SILVER SHADOW** BENTLEY **T-SERIES** — 978-1-845841-46-1

ISO **500 & 600** — 978-1-845841-47-8

JAGUAR **XJ-S** — 978-1-845841-61-4

SUBARU **IMPREZA** — 978-1-845841-63-8

BSA **Bantam** — 978-1-845841-65-2

VOLKSWAGEN **GOLF GTI** — 978-1-845841-88-1

Jaguar/Daimler **XJ40** — 978-1-845841-92-8

Jaguar/Daimler **XJ** — 978-1-845842-00-0

 **MINI** — 978-1-845842-04-8

FORD **CAPRI** — 978-1-845842-05-5

TRIUMPH **STAG** — 978-1-845842-70-3

Norton **Commando** — 978-1-845842-81-9

Peugeot **205 GTI** — 978-1-845842-83-3

Honda **SOHC FOURS** — 978-1-845842-84-0

Kawasaki **TRIPLES & FOURS** — 978-1-845842-87-1

BMW **Z3** — 978-1-845842-90-1

HARLEY-DAVIDSON **Big Twins** — 978-1-845843-03-8

HONDA **CBR FireBlade** — 978-1-845843-07-6

HONDA **CBR600 HURRICANE** — 978-1-845843-09-0

TRIUMPH **TR7 & TR8** — 978-1-845843-16-8

CORVETTE C2 — 978-1-845843-29-8

Porsche **911SC** — 978-1-845843-30-4

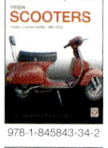 VESPA **SCOOTERS** — 978-1-845843-34-2

Porsche **911 (964)** — 978-1-845843-38-0

Porsche **911 (996)** — 978-1-845843-39-7

Porsche **911 (993)** — 978-1-845843-40-3

LAND ROVER **SERIES I, II & IIA** — 978-1-845843-48-9

MG **TD, TF & TF1500** — 978-1-845843-52-6

Austin **SEVEN** — 978-1-845843-53-3

MG/AUSTIN-HEALEY **MIDGET & SPRITE** — 978-1-845843-54-0

Triumph **Spitfire & GT6** — 978-1-845843-56-4

JAGUAR **XK8** — 978-1-845843-59-5

JAGUAR **Mark 1 & 2** — 978-1-845843-60-1

BMW **E21 3 Series** — 978-1-845843-66-3

MG **Replicas** — 978-1-845843-95-3

ALFA ROMEO GIULIA **GT COUPÉ** — 978-1-904788-69-0

 PORSCHE **928** — 978-1-904788-70-6

VOLKSWAGEN **BEETLE** — 978-1-904788-72-0

JAGUAR **E-type** 3.8 & 4.2 litre — 978-1-904788-85-0

ALFA ROMEO GIULIA **SPIDER** — 978-1-904788-98-0

£9.99*/$19.95*

*prices subject to change, p&p extra.
For more details visit www.veloce.co.uk
or email info@veloce.co.uk

For all things Jaguar across the globe

Keep your eye on the dream

A glimpse of perfection

www.Xclusively-Jaguar.com

Established 2008

Index